Simulation, Spectacle, and the Ironies of Education Reform

Critical Studies in Education and Culture Series

Simulation, Spectacle, and the Ironies of Education Reform

Guy Senese with Ralph Page

Foreword by Henry A. Giroux

Critical Studies in Education and Culture Series
Edited by Henry A. Giroux and Paulo Freire

BERGIN & GARVEY
Westport, Connecticut • London

Library of Congress Cataloging-in-Publication Data

Senese, Guy B.
    Simulation, spectacle, and the ironies of education reform / Guy
Senese with Ralph Page; foreword by Henry A. Giroux.
        p. cm. — (Critical studies in education and culture series,
    ISSN 1064–8615)
    Includes bibliographical references and index.
    ISBN 0–89789–402–2 (alk. paper). — ISBN 0–89789–444–8 (pbk.)
    1. Educational change—United States—Case studies. 2. Education—
United States—Aims and objectives—Case studies. 3. Educational
anthropology—United States—Case studies. I. Page, Ralph (Ralph
Cornell) II. Title. III. Series.
LA210.S392   1995
370′.973—dc20   94–38514

British Library Cataloguing in Publication Data is available.

Library of Congress Catalog Card Number: 94–38514
ISBN: 0–89789–402–2
        0–89789–444–8 (pbk.)
ISSN: 1064–8615

First published in 1995

Bergin & Garvey, 88 Post Road West, Westport, CT 06881
An imprint of Greenwood Publishing Group, Inc.

Printed in the United States of America

The paper used in this book complies with the
Permanent Paper Standard issued by the National
Information Standards Organization (Z39.48–1984).

10 9 8 7 6 5 4 3 2 1

Copyright Acknowledgments

The authors and publisher are grateful for permission to reprint excerpts from the following copyrighted sources:

Guy Senese, "Warnings on Resistance and the Language of Possibility: Gramsci and a Pedagogy from the Surreal," *Educational Theory* 41, no. 1 (Winter 1991): 13–23. Used by permission of *Educational Theory*.

Guy Senese, "Away from Goodness: The *Challenger* Disaster and the Paradoxes of a Nation at Risk," *Educational Foundations* 6, no. 3 (Summer 1992): 33–49. Used by permission of Caddo Gap Press.

In Memory of
I. S. and C. M.

Contents

Foreword

While it may sound harsh, the language that has dominated educational reform for the last fifteen years has not only failed to address the pressing problems of schooling and public life, it has also become insular and self-serving. Conservatives have consistently dominated the debate through a call for national standards, an appeal to improving workplace skills, and the attempt to convince schools and teachers to transmit a checklist of positive "family values" linked to upholding national identity, free enterprise, and constituted authority. Within this discourse, character becomes a market variable and cultural differences a deficit. Progressives on the other hand have recognized that students who are defined as working class, racial others, or outside the pale of heterosexual orientation experience severe forms of discrimination in America's schools. Unfortunately, when such groups argue that such discrimination is to be found not merely in the prejudice of teachers but in the very foundations of what is construed as legitimate curriculum knowledge, progressives seem both unprepared if not outright defensive.

Radical educators have not done much better. Of course, it is true that such educators have inserted into the discourse of educational

reform crucial considerations such as race, class, sexual orientation, and gender. But, these issues have often been taken up almost
solely within the limited language of criticism and have often been
rooted in internecine ideological struggles with other progressive
educators. What seemed like a promising educational reform
movement in the late 1970s appears largely to have degenerated
into a disparate movement confined to academic conferences and
the art of petty academic sniping. Unwilling to connect specific
criticisms to a broader project of reform, radical critics have
become virtually insignificant players in the current educational
reform debate.

What is so important about Guy Senese's book is that he
attempts to resurrect the language of criticism by refocusing it in
two strategic ways. First, he borrows from the language of popular
culture and everyday life to analyze how educational reform has
been trapped in the discourse of a reinvented technicism and
instrumentalism. Second, he connects the substance of his critiques,
whether they be of the *Challenger* space tragedy or the art of boxing
with an ethical discourse that takes the elimination of human
suffering and the empowerment of working-class students as its goal.

What is also striking in Senese's account is the way in which he
illuminates how excellence has become a code word to decouple
learning from compassion and school success from social justice.
Through an analysis of how Christa McAuliffe was treated before
and after her death in the *Challenger* explosion in the popular press
and official government pronouncements, Senese makes clear how
a dominant pedagogy can work to erase conflict, differences, and
a practical politics of care in its construction of national heroes,
public memory, and social identities. For Senese, the McAuliffe
tragedy embodied a larger catastrophe, a rampant technicism that
split reason from the body, empathy from risk taking, and vision
from achievement.

Central to *Simulation, Spectacle, and the Ironies of Education
Reform* is Senese's refusal to use traditional narrative structures,
tired metaphors, and the language of certainty. On the contrary,
Senese pushes language and a decentralized narrative structure to

its limits by connecting a seemingly odd mix of subjects such as boxing, Baudrillard, simulation, the Triangle Shirtwaist Company fire of 1911, surrealism, and the legacy of Paul Goodman. Through this extensive and spirited journey into a disparate metaphoric space, Senese constructs a fresh and original analysis of a changing capitalist order and its relationship to the symbolic and institutional structures of schooling.

In an attempt to retain critical pedagogy as a hope against hopelessness, Senese calls for educators to temper the language of possibility with a concrete sense of the cultural, economic, bureaucratic, and institutional conditions that stand in the way of social change. Attempting to resurrect the age-old question of what constitutes really useful education for working-class students, Senese works hard to link seemingly contradictory theoretical traditions such as the Frankfurt school, the surrealists, and Gramsci's "traditional" views on education. What emerges is a rigorous effort to rescue the critical moments of what Senese calls traditionalism as part of a dialectical struggle to fashion a radical discourse in which empowerment does not get reduced to the circus barker's call at the tent of opportunism, fraud, and spectacle.

Simulation, Spectacle, and the Ironies of Education Reform offers, with no apologies, a fresh critique and voice to the debates that have been conducted by educators over the last fifteen years. Challenging both the style and substance of these debates, Senese offers his own brand of representational politics and educational reform. For those readers who want to experience a roller-coaster ride through the rituals of critique and the rupturing discourse of indeterminacy, this is the place to begin.

—Henry A. Giroux

Acknowledgments

The greatest satisfaction I get from a project like this is looking back over the enjoyable associations which helped make it worthwhile. Many people have encouraged this project along the way and have made it an exciting journey. Ralph Page was an integral part of its inception and its conception. He has assisted and encouraged me over the last eight years, since the day we stood in the halls of the College of Education at the University of Illinois and discussed the shock of the *Challenger* disaster and what it might say about education reform that was itself burning like a house afire that year. It was one of many unforgettable conversations on the issues that unfold here. Without Ralph, this book would not have been written. That's not to say he agrees with everything I've written, so whatever problems the reader finds here, those were Ralph's ideas.

I'd like to acknowledge the following friends and colleagues for their help with materials, articles, criticism, or good conversation conducted in good faith on a group of what must have seemed strangely disparate subjects: Richard Angelo, Ron Dewar, Corrine Glesne, Betty Lahti, Mary Leach, Stuart McAninch, Wilma Miranda, Jeff Mirel, Judy Mogilka, Scott Mordecai, Kevin Owens,

Larry Parker, Tex Sherman, Steve Tozer, Carolyn White, and George Chicagouris, who with Laura Pacetti helped me as a student researcher. Thanks also to my sister, Christina Senese, who designed the cover for the paper edition. To Richard Brosio goes my gratitude for his encouragement, support, and careful criticism of earlier drafts. Thanks also to Glenn Smith, for a partial release from teaching responsibilities to complete the book, and to Lynn Flint and HenryA. Giroux for their generous and careful efforts to help this unfold.

Special thanks to my wife, Jamie, for her reading and comments on previous drafts, and to her and our children, Mia and Zoë, for their support and love.

Finally, I dedicate this work to both the memory of my mother— my best teacher—Ida Senese, and to Christa McAuliffe, in the hope for a more proper memory of the meaning of her work, the depth of her courage, and the tragedy for which she is remembered.

Simulation, Spectacle, and the Ironies of Education Reform

1

Introduction: Education Reform and the Law of the Conservation of Suffering

This book is focused on reform as a ritual of rehabilitation. It is an attempt to tell a few tales that circulate around the most recent education reform discussions and that magnify myths of rehabilitation while they demonstrate what is obscured by reform dialogue. As it turns out, the bizarre and confusing refraction of the current conditions in emerging global economic order creates strange effects. As such, I wind up telling orderly stories of changing events, which read like a tabloid.

This is written as part of the dialogue among educators concerning the chances for progressive educational emancipation under current conditions of neoconservative retrenchment, a collapsing welfare state, and an ongoing polemic calling for public-school and public-sector reforms fit for a changing global political-economic order.

The cases that follow are disjointed in time and space but related in theme and mythic dimensions. The first is about Christa McAuliffe's participation in the *Challenger* shuttle "teacher in space" mission. It presents her story as she became the embodiment of the high-tech teacher-savior for global economic and military competition and educational reform as the linchpin for that. The second is a story of the world of boxing's mythic struggles and its ongoing effort to maintain stature and social hygiene through reforms. The themes of upward mobility and free competition resound like a ring bell in any boxing tale, and its reality and its reforms sound with similar resonance when one listens closely. The last of the case studies is a tale of work—or what is left of it in the late twentieth century in America—the Hawthorne telephone factory and its fate, relative to global economic change.

Oddly, these cases, wholly different in many ways, are convergent. They each separately embody themes of human emancipation at the core of the twentieth-century American drama. Space, sports, and business—each have become archetypes of transcendence, assuming mythic proportions.

So we get from them resounding themes—the American dream of upward social mobility through corporeal struggle—in the ring, through science and applied technology, and through sophisticated "human resource" management in business. These images range from the sublime to the ridiculous, to a sense of the tabloid: "Engineers Make Exploding Rocket—Put People In"; "School Teacher Dies in Mission to Outer Space"; "Doctors Say Boxing Safe, Suggest Use as Cure for Poverty"; "World's Most Successful Telephone Factory Spontaneously Implodes!"

If there is something weird here, even something ghoulish, it is, I believe, the flip side of a sacrament, a sacrament gone wrong. There is, indeed, something of a forced sacredness to the incantations of reform. In *The Human Condition*, Hannah Arendt presents her argument for the centrality of Space, Sport, and Work in any calculus of salvation for an ostensibly secular polity.[1] While we have highlighted the seriousness of these ideas, their centrality as a focus for rehabilitative ritual has been understudied.

A fundamental part of reform is sacrifice. Perhaps this is where it becomes sacramental. Rebounding back and forth as themes in these cases, violent sacrifice appear again and again: the loss of Christa McAuliffe and her subsequent image as the model for the "excellence" movement, the suffering at the base of the spectacle of boxing, the natural sacrifice of workers' privacy, control, and, ultimately, their jobs, through the history of Hawthorne. If there is any order emerging here, it seems to be a first law of the conservation of suffering.

In his study of ritual in Catholic schools, Peter McLaren talks about schooling as a "culture of pain." He states, "Pain, whether existential or physical, is intimately connected to the pedagogic encounter."[2] He uncovers some important ways schooling rides on the symbology of its complicated presentations, and analyzes in detail how these symbols manifest themselves in the smallest gestures. These rituals embody "dominant metaphors of the social structure and, when exposed, reveal latent connections between themselves and the preservation of inequality, despite the ideology of equal educational opportunity."[3]

McLaren describes one particularly pointed irony—the Catholic school exploitation of the image of Christ, whose own suffering is highlighted, reconverting his iconography from a defender of peace to a "silent accomplice in acts of symbolic violence." He suggests "an approach to school reform that takes into account structure and symbolic agency."[4] I think that ritual has an important location beyond the classroom microcosm. If there is something sacramental in the routine gestures of the schoolroom, and if there is likewise a sense of the purely formal in the rites of credentialism, the larger motion of social and educational reform dialogues reflect a similar incantatory aspect.

Almost like an encyclical, the *Nation At Risk* report generated reforms by the nearly supernatural appeal of federal edict. That the reforms which followed had nothing to do with the problems they were trying to solve—the fading American economy—would be interesting enough. What is more intriguing is their power to distract and redirect our perception regarding appropriate educational goals.

It is no secret that this latest spasm of reform occurred during a retrenchment of probusiness, antiwelfare state of resurgent capitalist ideology. What is less widely acknowledged in the mainstream commercial and educational presses was how its reaction worked to plug a leaking dike of economic crisis and legitimation problems with global capitalism.

The case studies in this book are followed by a reflection on some of the most cogent responses to both the 1980s reform movement with its neoconservative mouthpieces and to the rigidities of Left theory which lay paralyzed in its inability to theorize beyond structural domination of schooling. The "language of possibility" of Henry Giroux and colleagues argued for an open space, a path to democratic agency which was pioneered by the "new sociologists" of education and mapped out by critical ethnographers. Many of these theorists have hinted at the problem of subjectivity formation, but underargued its enormity. I hope this book is not an attempt to overargue it, but aims at a clearer estimation of the task for critical education.

The very way reform rhetoric was able to sweep the country into a redesign of its credential market is itself one iteration of the power of capital to saturate structures of ideological formation, even among the class of traditional intellectuals. If democracy can grow in the cracks between the imperatives of capital and the ossification of working-class consciousness, critical educators must mobilize the manifestations of resistance, which often mimic school pathologies, so argued the theorists of possibility.

Massumi comments on Deleuze and Guattari, noting their argument that current conditions threaten to close any cracks open for such agency. In a shifting global marketplace, organized by mass media, where legitimate democratic public spaces are drained like Faustian swamps for the hypercolonization by marketeers, "subjectivity becomes isomorphic to capital."[5] The triumph of neoconservatism, renaming democracy for new ends, reminds us of what may come in the renewed ideological warfare against the working classes.

Massumi argues that capitalism still relies on "institutions to open bodies to it, to make them susceptible to its magic." Neoconservatism has won triumphs in redirecting the blame for economic failure to the schools, by imploding welfare-state supports and by making America safe for privilege. It has purified the identity of liberalism and capitalism. "It is the coming out of capital, a new golden age of greed that dares to say its name."[6]

The American working class and the public-school students can no longer, in the global saturation of capital, hitch a ride on an economy whose success depends on American market domination of both production and consumption. Indeed, as Giroux and Aronowitz noted, "unless one can project growth levels that exceed productivity gains, the prospect for a new surge in employment is exceedingly doubtful . . . unlike the postwar period, the United States no longer has free reign in capital and commodity markets."[7] Although written in 1986, the conditions in the current "recovery," of wealthy stockholders seeing their shares rise in value while American unemployment figures stagnate, make this statement prescient.

The mystification of the consequences of the capitalist business cycle and its impact on ersatz reform politics should concern educators. However, a more directly pedagogical issue emerges from a description of the depth of consciousness saturation by postindustrial capitalist imperatives. Educators must be alert to traditions within critical intellectual scholarship that speak to the condition where socialization, as *suppression* of the imaginary, is renamed as education and the means by which the imaginary takes over the ego is renamed as "learning."[8]

The last chapters of this book are contemplations on the traditions of intellect and potential eduction that may be defended in an increasingly instrumental, anti-intellectual *renaming* of educational vocation in our time. The entire book owes much to what I believe are the clearest descriptions of the current crisis, the anti-instrumentalism of the Frankfurt school thinkers, and the anti-pedagogies of surrealism. I only claim participation in the nascent "cultural studies" movement, which has borrowed from both traditions, by my willingness to plunder any source to create stories that must be judged, in part, by their aesthetic success. If anything, these are studies in a wilderness, a wilderness that is unnatural as it requires colonization of the minds that created it, by the totalizing desires of capitalist saturation.[9]

As such, I am forced to live with the unpleasant feeling that what Baudrillard has suggested is correct—official reason has finally

fallen in on itself. We who admired authentic progressive goals have
had to sift for the remnants of them in a clutter of simulations—
mock free markets, fake ladders of opportunity—ersatz salvation
through the glory of honest work. And we must do this all—to
revive something truly sacred in the human project, from within
the remnants of those public institutions, schools and universities,
whose promises for salvation have worn thin, for an increasingly
disoriented public quickly losing its taste for democracy. "Pedagogy
vanishes except of form, because there are no more experts."[10]

Horkheimer and Adorno have shown how we still require
slavery for the emancipation of the leisure class. They correctly
identified the problem of critical subjectivity in a world where
instrumental, technical reason had not only allowed but made
possible the horrors of twentieth-century violence. It is true that
critical ethnography has highlighted the ambiguous relationship
between the working class and hegemonic institutions. However,
that ambiguous relationship and the "resistance" that manifests
itself in real or symbolic violence among public-school students is
also showing the potential in every capitalist "democracy" for a
critically dangerous alliance between capitalist officials and
working-class enforcers, in a reemerging antidemocratic despotism,
a new fist of state capital in the velvet glove of liberalism.

Critical ethnographers, I believe, must learn to live with the fact
that in school violence and "resistance" they did not discover the
seeds of critical reason, but the birth of a postindustrial fascism—
and one that might grow to make Middletown look like New
Harmony. In the search for educational values commensurate with
the obstacles of this period, I am reminded of Marcuse's argument
that values worth the name are based on our sense for the suffering
of others.[11] He would ask for a radical negation of the "performance principle" in the construction of educational goals.[12]

The final section of this work describes some pedagogic-academic
conditions that follow in the direction of studies-for-compassion,
the kind of compassion intimated by Marcuse, and for an intellect
forged as an end in itself, not as a means to an end. It searches for
a "soul development" that works not to fashion "individuals"

to perform in the world, but to make a world worthy of their humanity.

Thomas McCarthy, following Block and Benjamin, causes us to question again the "production of cultural goods as spoils that the ruling elite carries in its triumphal parade and so the process of tradition as to be disentangled from myth."[13] Without an education that is an engagement in the myth structures implied in canonical curriculum and traditional schooling, "suspicion cannot help but arise that an emancipation without happiness and lacking in fulfillment might be just as possible as relative prosperity without the elimination of oppression."[14]

This book becomes a collection of impressions on education reform as a cultural movement and political spectacle of the 1980s. It is one with strong ritual rhetoric where emancipation appears like magic from a constricting political economic reality; where working-class emancipation, the myth of bourgeois liberalism must now be pulled, ill-borne, like a pigeon from a magician's coat.

Daniel Cottom's bizarre but fascinating look at nineteenth-century spiritualism illustrates the weird innards of this argument. Like recent educational reformism, late nineteenth-century spiritualists made the most trivial objects—tables, chairs—resound with portentous significance.[15] Radical education critics have responded to education reformism in much the same way as critics of spiritualism did. "Spiritualism was suspect because it was bending discourse into forms at once bizarre and reassuring."[16] Education reform, not quite as bizarre as levitating tables, is used as evidence of the "other world." But consider claims that unsold inventories, stagnant stock prices, and market saturation were due to a half-point drop in a nationally administered test of culture-facts. Bizarre and in many ways *more* reassuring to politicians, government bureaucrats, bankers, brokers, and other assorted elites for whom any discourse bent in the service of capital legitimation was welcome wisdom. This is the new wisdom, and to paraphrase André Breton, *your* wisdom is words moving in *my* service. What follows is an effort to illustrate this.

NOTES

1. Hannah Arendt, *The Human Condition* (New York: Doubleday, 1959).

2. Peter McLaren, *Schooling as a Ritual Performance* (London: Routledge & Kegan Paul, 1986), p. 13.

3. Ibid., p. 27.

4. Ibid., p. 13.

5. Brian Massumi, *A User's Guide to "Capitalism and Schizophrenia"* (Cambridge: MIT Press, 1992), p. 135.

6. Ibid., p. 131.

7. Stanley Aronowitz and Henry A. Giroux, *Education under Siege* (South Hadley, Mass.: Bergin & Garvey, 1985), p. 194.

8. Ibid., p. 19.

9. For a good perspective on this developing scholarship, see Fred Inglis, *Cultural Studies* (Oxford: Blackwell, 1993).

10. Aronowitz and Giroux, *Education under Siege*, p. 66.

11. Jurgen Habermas, "Psychic Thermador and the Birth of Rebellious Subjectivity," in Richard J. Bernstein, ed., *Habermas and Modernity* (Cambridge: MIT Press, 1985), pp. 68–77, p. 77.

12. Ibid., p. 67.

13. Albrecht Wellmer, "Reason, Utopia, and *The Dialectic of Enlightenment*," in Bernstein, *Habermas*, pp. 35–66, p. 48.

14. Thomas McCarthy, "Reflections on Rationalization in *The Theory of Communicative Action*," in Bernstein, *Habermas*, pp. 176–191, p. 188.

15. Daniel Cottom, *Abyss of Reason: Cultural Movements, Revelations, and Betrayals* (Oxford: Oxford University Press, 1991), p. 28.

16. Ibid., p. 37.

2

Away from Goodness: The *Challenger* Disaster and the Irony of a Nation at Risk

If the teacher in space doesn't come back to teach, something's wrong.

Christa McAuliffe, teacher[1]

I was asked, yes, at that point in time I was asked to quantify my concerns, and I said I couldn't. I couldn't quantify it. I had no data to quantify it, but I did say that it was away from goodness in the current data base.

Roger Boisjoly, engineer, Morton-Thiokol[2]

Space is the place.

Sun Ra, musician[3]

No one who saw it will likely forget the *Challenger* explosion of January 28, 1986. For educators, such as myself, the event takes on special meaning since one of our own died as a result of that disastrous chain of events leading to the explosion of that afternoon. While we remember it, the subsequent coverage of the event has, in crucial ways, taught us to remember the loss of Christa McAuliffe, the "teacher in space," for many of the wrong reasons.

Linked to the education reform movement of the 1980s, McAuliffe's participation on *Challenger* was an important building block in the Reagan administration's effort to publicize its commitment to a linkage between high-technology/national security considerations and the new reform. Like many aspects of the reform movement itself, McAuliffe's participation in the mission was a star-crossed effort, with more rhetorical than legitimate meaning.

Yet the swirl of rhetoric has obscured the fact that McAuliffe's senseless death is emblematic of the extent to which the instrumental uses of education have come to predominate in the current reform climate. I will discuss how, for example, the failure of the shuttle, like the failure of the American industrial enterprise, is remembered as a technical problem (faulty O-rings) which has a technical solution, when the deep meaning of the disaster is the breakdown of industrial democracy, and the weakness of will to face real problems in light of short-term financial pressures.

This study is intended to let the story of the *Challenger* shed light on the character and ideals of American public education. The *Challenger* accident, while widely understood as further proof of our "rising tide of mediocrity" is, in fact, further proof of how far we have drifted from democratic ideals and from the importance of an education that prepares the way for and embodies the ideals of criticism and free inquiry. Furthermore, the fact that this could be so easily lost on the public at large is further evidence of the power of ideology to reify false constructs in favor of a convenient national amnesia concerning what is truly "at risk" in this nation.

Of all the sour elements that came from the era of 1980s education reform, nothing, in my estimation, parallels the injustice done to Christa McAuliffe or to the vocation which her shuttle participation was intended to glorify. She has been made the namesake of dozens of technology-in-education awards, given honor as a hero of education reform, and her name has been used to promote the very educational impulse that her untimely death should have been used to question—the notion that this nation is "at risk" because of a failure of competitiveness. Nothing could be further from the truth. The *Challenger* becomes, at once, an argument of calculation and a mythological venture. It went up like a great grim roman candle, and as it exploded, inscribed a great Y in the blue Florida sky—Y—Why? So sharp in memory, because it was doomed. So Roman in its service to an imploding empire.

The metaphor of the *Challenger* gives access to a critique and analysis of the contradictions between the symbol of the *Challenger* and the teacher in space and the actual character of educational enterprise as an adjunct of the state in the 1980s reform climate. This is an opportunity to follow Douglas Kellner's advice to uncover an historical episode in a synthesis of social theory and cultural critique.[4]

This symbolic analysis employs methods from Ellul and Arendt, in their emphasis on the power of propaganda and bureaucracy to structure reason in the service of authoritarian purposes.[5] The study employs methods suggested by Baudrillard's analysis of simulation and society, and Breton's liberatory methods of change through surrealism, by suggesting the need to recover the power of the symbolic as an intellectually liberatory force.[6]

FAME AND EXPLOITATION

Christa McAuliffe was born on September 2, 1948, to Edward and Grace Corrigan in Boston, the oldest of five children. One account of her life asks us to visualize Christa as a child in 1961 watching the first American space flight, remarking to a classmate that she wished she could go up there too. She was chosen for her ability to represent the space program and carry its educational message. Her fame was precisely the result of her characteristic as an exemplar for the ordinary American teacher.

From the beginning the *Challenger* mission attempted to capitalize on the high profile of education reform which was then in full swing. Francis (Dick) Scobee, the mission commander, would comment that "no matter what happens on this mission, it's going to be known as the teacher mission. We feel that's good, because people will remember what we do." [7] It would not be too strong to say that the best values of the teaching profession were exploited for the purposes of advertising the education reform movement and using its momentum to mobilize support for the space program in the bargain. In the first place, Christa McAuliffe had no function on the shuttle beyond her responsibility to advertise it and the purposes of education reform. The campaign to put a teacher in space was "part of NASA's continuing public relations effort to create space stars to help win national and international support— and more congressional funding—for the shuttle program."[8] It was also partly the result of the Reagan administration trying to appeal to a "hostile teacher's union, [and who] during his re-election campaign, pledged that the first citizen passenger would be a teacher."[9] The nation had first heard of the idea of putting a teacher in space, the first true civilian astronaut, in Ronald Reagan's 1985 State of the Union address.

This program is emblematic of the ironic, intensified de-professionalization of teaching that accompanied the rhetoric of the 1980s education reform. In the heart of the educational excellence movement, Christa was selected despite what was termed a "weak résumé" compared to the other ten finalists. Her selection was in great part based on her possession of "the intangibles: she was wholesome, a churchgoer, a jogger, a mother of two . . . she was even pretty."[10] Significantly, of the ten finalists only two were teachers of mathematics or science. There was clearly no effort to bring actual expertise into space; rather the effort was to select, through a veritable talent show, the person who could seem most like the archetypal reform era teacher.

The hyperbole of the reform years has obscured the actual work lives many teachers experience. Despite the obstacles to their curricular and methodological control, as they always have, many good teachers have used stealth and quiet determination to maintain their professional integrity. Despite the NASA perception of her "weak" résumé, Christa McAuliffe's quiet resistance to the alienating demands of the "talent contest" and her subsequent activities on the shuttle becomes clear. In one of her interviews she says, "I think the reason I went into teaching was because I wanted to make an impact on other people and to have that impact on myself. I think I learn sometimes as much from my students as they learn from me."[11] Yet, despite what was to be her growing insistence that she be represented for who she is and what she does as a teacher, the overarching imperatives of the "show" were to subsume her resistance to being used as a showpiece. It also undermined her or anyone else's ability to determine the extent of the real risks that were developing. And the show would go on.

On July 29, 1985, Christa would watch nervously with the rest of the nation, as the *Challenger* on an earlier flight would be required to abort after an engine failure. She would console herself in an interview: "Just think of those early astronauts in those capsules who had no buttons to push. They had no control over their destiny if something went wrong. Today's program is a very safe program, so I'm not nervous. I'd just like them to get all the kinks out of it before I get on it."[12] Later, on the day of that interview, Roger Boisjoly, an engineer for Morton-Thiokol, Inc., the company that manufactured the shuttle's booster rockets, wrote a memo to senior management warning of problems in the O-rings, the rubber, and putty seals between the solid rocket booster's field joints. "It is my honest and very real fear," he wrote, "that if we do not take immediate action to dedicate a team to solve the problem . . . then we stand in jeopardy of losing a flight, along with all the launch pad facilities, . . . The result would be a catastrophe of the highest order—loss of human life."[13] Robert Hohler notes, ironically, that, "Christa knew nothing about the memo. She knew only that the *Challenger* was safely in orbit and that in less than twenty-four hours she faced her most rigorous test of the summer— a visit with Johnny Carson." She was being primed as the biggest advertising coup of the space agency's history. Carson, in the sweet manner he usually reserved for child stars, kindly suggested Christa's real function: "I think NASA made a very good choice, because I think you can communicate this to most of us who really can't understand all of it. You're really excited to go, huh?"[14]

All during her preparation as a double-duty advertisement for the shuttle program and education reform, Christa steadily protested her assigned role as space actress. She often clashed with the education coordinator, Robert Mayfield, a "science teacher from Texas who chafed at working with a social studies teacher from New Hampshire."[15] "It would be a lot easier if she knew science," he had argued. According to Hohler, Mayfield and McAuliffe did not speak the same vocabulary, and "worse, the science demonstrations excited Mayfield the most and meant the least to Christa." She was interested in the implications of her participation as a social studies teacher.[16] She wanted to teach the televised lessons her way. When asked to read a scripted lesson, she refused, saying, "This isn't a stage play, . . . teachers don't need speeches. All they need is a lesson plan and their students. It's worked for ages on Earth, and there's no reason why it shouldn't work up there."[17] The fact that a history teacher was chosen in a talent contest to teach a scripted science lesson in outer space tells much about the lack of seriousness in the "teacher in space" project and about the twisted meaning of professionalization in the era of 1980s reform.

ADVERTISING

While Christa avoided the script, she could not see the part she was playing in a long-standing space commercial campaign. In "Selling the Moon: The U.S. Manned Space Program and the Triumph of Commodity Scientism," Michael L. Smith argues that the manned "space project's social function and presentation techniques approximated those of the most highly developed communication medium in American culture: advertising."[18] Christa became a part of the long line of image-making techniques to enhance the palatability of the space program. Like other scientific advances, capable of drifting behind what Marcuse called the "technological veil," the government space agency and the media both depended on the arousal of human interest to project importance on a policy whose benefits were obscure and whose entertainment value was limited to the short-lived thrill of watching people in puffy suits of Reynolds wrap tumbling stiffly through a void.

The American public had grown used to the perception that technology was justified in part by its entertainment value and in

part by its ability to fulfill the promise of a better life. "For Cape
Canaveral as well as Madison Avenue, the task was to link certain
public expectations of technology with the product or event in
question."[19] One prominent feature of both the revolutions in
aviation and advertising was the appearance of what Michael
Smith has called the "helmsman" image. Smith argues that Charles
Lindbergh was the first prominent helmsman developed in this
century to bring legitimation to any product or process. The Leo
Burnett company's invention of the ruggedly independent Marlboro
Man is another example of this concept paving the way for the
creation of the "astronaut."[20] The astronaut provided the required
personalization of space, despite the fact that space science could
proceed quite well in an automated form. However, this is a space
whose uses were increasingly being identified with the conquest
of *conceptual* territory, in the absence of the ability to conquer real
space during a very tense but very "cold" war.

Christa McAuliffe, while not the classic helmsman, has clearly
been put in the service of an image of personalized, domesticated
space, which, like all other space efforts, was argued to bring benefits
unconnected to the actual mission. Educational "excellence" was
supported for its tangential connection to the long-range goal of
increased productivity in a competitive "postindustrial" economy.
Thus was the teacher in space only tangentially connected to the
flight. She became an archetypal "helmsperson," like her earth-
bound counterpart, full-time wife and mother, full-time teacher; a
space domestic, who would project the sharp American "lady
teacher" image around the world. While she resisted all the image-
mongering, she was still shaped to personalize both space and
education reform in one deft "ad-age" stroke. Her projected image
appears here to support an illusion of rugged individualism that, if
Horkheimer was correct, was required to provide moral and ideological support, while the independent economic subject was being
eliminated in commodity-drunk late capitalism. Richard Brosio
reminds us how Horkheimer, Marcuse, and other Frankfurt school
theorists highlighted how instrumental reason cut the deep rift
between science and ethics. This rift is no better illustrated than

by an examination of image and metaphor imbedded in state-dominated military and scientific technology.[21] Had McAuliffe lived, Warhol might have made her image into wallpaper.

At the same time that reform reports were highlighting the industrial productivity failures and blaming them on mediocre education, the shuttle program was under similar pressure to demonstrate its own productivity. There was increased pressure to produce more launches, more efficiently, and on a tight schedule. Martin Carnoy has shown how deceptive was the call for productivity increases in the context of high-tech industry.[22] What might result in a high-quality education for the research and development class making up the preproduction end of this revolution might just as well result in a mediocre standard set for that class engaged in the production end of the microelectronics industry and in the burgeoning service sector of the so-called flexible economy.

Christine Shea highlights the nature of the contradictions of education reform, obscuring the class conflict inherent in it. Indeed the call for equity and excellence—higher performance standards for all—is curious given that the global marketplace and multinational corporations are dismembering the traditional source of working-class jobs. The craft/industrial center is being redistributed globally. Unquestioned allegiance to the high-tech labor force and higher performance standards will work to impoverish the growing white-collar working class through increased interclass job competition and lower salaries, and to further disempower the secondary service labor force.[23]

Quality products and a quality education for their design are only part of the reform story. The other part is the increase in sales promotion of a shoddy shuttle product based on deception, image making, and managerial slave-driving of overworked engineers. The shuttle embodies high-quality science, engineering expertise, and image-advertisement driven prerogatives that bordered on bathos. In this case, "sales" are shuttle launches, a sale based on the image, the pitch, and the close.

PROPAGANDA

In remembering the *Challenger* explosion I am struck by the memory of the incredible violence of the explosion. It seemed at that time that minor things went wrong often: an oxygen leak, a computer malfunction, those delays and inconveniences we became used to. For the shuttle to simply disintegrate, blow up, was unthinkable, almost ludicrous. What followed this extremity was televised silence, and where there was not silence, there was only the crackle of NASA jargon: "We have negative contact,—loss of downlink" "There appears to be a major malfunction" and so on. It is in the intersection of violence, bureaucratic language, and myth that the full meaning of this event might teach us yet if we look.

Not since the moon landings had so many people been turned to a space launch as they were for the *Challenger.* "From the Virgin Islands to an Eskimo village in the Arctic Circle, they waited—two and a half million students and their teachers, among them Christa's colleagues and most of the class of 51-L. . . . One of the finalists, Charlie Sposato's, class prepared for the launch by studying Stanley Kubrick's *2001: A Space Odyssey.*"[24] *Dr. Strangelove* might have been more appropriate for the events that would unfold.

The effects of this disastrous event and its aftermath are elegantly described by an application of Jacques Ellul's venerable but sturdy propaganda model. Ellul showed how subtle and flexible propaganda can be as an expression of totalizing State objectives.[25] Ellul argued that propaganda has become necessary, in much the same way that advertising has. It is not a stream of false information produced to deceive. It is rather a managerial tool used to interpret reality for the masses. As such, it acts to streamline a potentially "chaotic" political or consumer response. Since production depends on orderly information management, management is required; chaos is counterproductive.[26]

For Ellul, propaganda is necessary in the exercise of secretive power. Information control and image making are essential to

ensure predictable political outcomes, to establish resilient belief
structures, and to manage public responses. A glance at some of
the press releases and magazine treatments just after the explosion
reveals something of the controlled uses of information which,
characteristically, made the major news media impotent to objec-
tively study the situation when their main role had occupied them,
in the months prior to launch, as boosters for the Teacher-in-Space
Club. At that time, Steve Daley of the *Chicago Tribune* wrote a
newspaper column called "On Television." In this he noted how
"despite the drama, despite a steadfast effort all day long, as the
networks waited for the promise of a late-afternoon news conference from the National Aeronautics and Space Administration
(NASA), it could likewise be argued that never had more network
air time been filled with less information."[27] Daley quotes ABC's
Peter Jennings, "If it sounds as if we're blathering on, it's because
we are waiting for some word from NASA."[28]

We will always have with us the image of the exploded shuttle.
We will also have the image of the media aftermath. We must live
with the uncomfortable image of the media as servant of the State,
waiting, "blathering," while another State agency prepares the
official response which would become news. What we would hear
from NASA would be the beginning of the construction of the
Challenger myth, and Christa McAuliffe would remain on stage
as the lead character, not in the tragedy it was, but in a travel
adventure. Malcolm McConnell has noted the "media love affair
with the man-in-space adventure."[29] He cites William Booth's
analysis of the NASA-media relationship which "details the media's
infatuation with the space shuttle . . . dazzled by the space agency's
image of technological brilliance, . . . space reporters spared
NASA the thorough scrutiny that might have improved chances of
averting a tragedy."[30] McConnell argues that it was NASA's
bureaucratic evasiveness and duplicity that led the press off the
trail of problems that were developing.

Ellul argues that propaganda must be able to "furnish an explanation for all happenings, a key to understand the whys and the
reasons for economic and political developments."[31] Indeed,

propaganda and bureaucracy are bedfellows in the development of this disaster. Propaganda need not be activated in the absence of an official need. In the case of the *Challenger*, the offices of NASA; Morton-Thiokol, the contractor; and the Marshall Space Flight Center, working somewhat in concert, protecting their prerogatives, made possible the attenuation of information, the propaganda that led to the tragedy. As early as 1978, John Q. Miller, Marshall's chief of the solid rocket booster project wrote memoranda that stated that the design of the field joints and O-ring assembly was "so hazardous that it could produce hot gas leaks and resulting catastrophic failure."[32] The problem had been noted at least *eight* years before the "accident," yet this was covered up in the effort to proceed smoothly. In November, 1981, the orbiter *Columbia* was discovered to have badly eroded field joints after flight. Marshall director Dr. William Lucas's people decided to keep the problem within the confines of the Marshall/Morton-Thiokol reporting channels, and away from the national space shuttle office in Houston and the associate administrator in Washington.[33] Lucas himself, as the single-minded taskmaster of the project, appears as Ellul's "monolithic individual. . . . [who will] have rationalizations not only for past actions, but for the future as well. He marches forward with full assurance of his righteousness. He is formidable in his equilibrium, all the more so because it is very difficult to break his harness of justifications."[34]

Ellul's model emphasizes that propaganda can effectively rest on a claim that some "fact is *untrue* which may actually *be true* but is difficult to prove."[35] The dangers present in the shuttle field joint design were present but "difficult to prove." This difficulty would be compounded in the bureaucratic political pressure which NASA had placed on itself. The launch productivity pressure was particularly great on the day of the disaster. NASA had included a contribution to the president's State of the Union address, which was intended for him to read as a rapt audience watched the shuttle whirl in orbit, waiting for its lesson from space the next morning. It read in part, "Tonight, while I am speaking to you, a young elementary school teacher [*sic*, she was not an elementary school teacher] from Concord, New Hampshire, is taking us all on the ultimate field trip as she orbits the Earth as the first citizen passenger on the space shuttle."[36] The speech promoted the space program and connected its imperatives with the "bright tomorrow that high technology would bring to increasingly stable and prosperous American families. . . . Christa McAuliffe epitomized this optimistic theme."[37] Indeed, Christa unwittingly became a surrogate propagandist. She is the "middle-class recruit" Ellul deemed necessary for the appropriate communicative power. In this she is not unlike the host of mid-American farm boys, the John Glenns and Neil Armstrongs, whose helmsmanship was so essential to the communication of this process toward a middle American audience.[38] The accessibility of these helmspersons as models satisfies the persistent need of mass man to connect, to alleviate the loneliness and isolation of contemporary life. People need, due to their alienation, to "believe and obey, to create and hear fables, to communicate in the language of myths."[39]

Indeed, the myth of the fallen hero, the only ill fate that can befall a helmsman, was continued in the moments after the explosion, and helped to manage its political impact. This modern tragedy rests not with the hero's tragic flaw, but in the machine's. McAuliffe's is almost a surreal presence reassuring our acquiescence. Rather than a helmsperson in control of her fate, she became the high-tech, white-collar, working-class citizen who was to symbolize the quintessential techno-serf.

The surrealists had suggested the liberatory potential in these kinds of "bizarre juxtapositions" and how our chance contact with an external object may remind us of ourselves, more than anything that takes place in the impoverished life of our conscious will. The obscene Y in the sky, the presence of a teacher in space, of all places, gives us the opportunity, if we take it, to catapult out of the vast network of "pseudo-satisfactions that make up the market system."[40] Her image managers might have said "she's not an astronaut but she plays one on TV" and valorize her participation by video caveat. We may, in a split second, see the absurdity in calling this explosion an accident. André Breton was convinced that we must take the opportunity to see the importance of chance and the automatic to reveal the outlines of our chains.[41] By the first anniversary of the disaster, we were being asked to observe a period of silence for the astronauts who "paid the ultimate price for the *mistakes* of others."[42] Duplicity would become "mistakes," ill-designed O-rings, a cheater's proof of our technological unpreparedness. A year after the explosion *Aviation Week and Space Technology* would argue, "The emphasis has to be on correcting the design deficiencies in the shuttle system . . . without diminishing the importance of the ceremony; however, care must be taken not to dwell on the *Challenger* loss to the point that it reopens old wounds or turns the anniversary observance into a time of recriminations, renewed criticism of NASA, or calls for the United States to abandon its efforts to conquer the space frontier."[43] This reminds us of the wider effort to shape public perceptions regarding the meaning of the disaster. We are reminded that the task of memory is to reinforce how the shuttle *failure* must be understood as part of the phenomenon which *had it succeeded*, would also have advertised the need for better high-technology products and processes.

BUREAUCRACY AND VIOLENCE

The *Challenger* incident is a story which reflects the nature of truth in a bureaucratic culture. Charles Peters identifies the shuttle's problems in the heart of several intertwined bureaucratic cultures: at Morton-Thiokol, Marshall Space Flight Center, and at NASA. Bureaucracies and the propaganda they generate become the locus for the development of pertinent information. Hannah Arendt's brilliant analysis of violence leads us back along the path of bureaucratic propaganda, to a place where information creates no truth, and where no one may be held responsible for the evil that lies generate. The inevitability of the violent shuttle explosion and the silence that followed are an emblem of her analysis. Bureaucracy, she wrote, is the "rule of an intricate system of bureaus in which no men, neither one nor the best, neither the few nor the many, can be held responsible, and which could be properly called rule by Nobody ... rule by Nobody is clearly the most tyrannical of all, since there is no one left who could even be asked to answer for what was being done."[44]

Arendt wanted to make distinction between power and violence. She said that power is more closely related to authority, where those in control have the assumed respect of the ruled. Power becomes violence when it assumes a completely instrumental character. The "implements of violence, like all other natural tools are designed and used for the purpose of multiplying natural strength until, in the last stage of their development, they can substitute for it."[45] Violence is power used in the absence of vested authority.

The uses of propaganda by themselves assume no particularly violent character. However, in the case of the shuttle disaster, we may witness a process of incremental rationalization, in which bureaucracy serves to mobilize this instrument of the space program, its machines and techniques further away from democratic accountability. Bureaucracy becomes the conduit for the development of power used in the absence of vested authority. The so-called shuttle "accident" embodies this definition of violence.

Peters writes an account of the nature of this process. He notes that the bad "news" of shuttle design flaws simply lost its power as information, because it ran counter to the logic of productivity which had come to dominate the program. Engineers "felt it was their job to solve problems, not burden the boss with them."[46] Peters quotes Paul Cloutier, a professor of space physics, "the game NASA is playing is the maximum tonnage per year at the minimum costs possible," and also quotes a *Newsweek* report that states, "some high officials don't want to hear about problems."[47] Peters' analysis is consistent with Ellul's discussion of leadership personality. "Every organization has a tendency to believe its own PR—NASA's walls are lined with glamorizing posters and photographs of the shuttle and other space machines—and usually the top man is the most thoroughly seduced because, after all, it reflects the most glory on him."[48] Peters goes on to cite the pressure NASA put on itself by encouraging the president's people to include a teacher-in-space reference in his State of the Union address. "NASA officials must have feared they were about to lose a PR opportunity of stunning magnitude, an opportunity to impress not only the media and the public but the agency's two most important constituencies, the White House and the Congress. Wouldn't you feel pressure to get that launch off this morning so that the President could talk about it tonight?"[49]

NASA's George Hardy is described telling Thiokol engineers who were terrified at the effect of this cold weather on field joint integrity, that he was, "appalled by their verbal recommendation that the launch be postponed. . . . Thiokol, which Hardy well knew was worried about losing its shuttle contract, was in effect being told, 'don't tell me' or 'don't tell me officially so I won't have to pass bad news along and my bosses will have deniability.' "[50] Peters argues the pivotal role played by bureaucracy in bringing on the violence embodied in this disaster.[51]

Engineer Roger Boisjoly reported that Morton-Thiokol's management style would not let anything compete or interfere with "the production and shipping of its boosters. The result was a program which gave the appearance of being controlled, while actually collapsing from within."[52] "Engineers were forbidden to speak up at Thiokol meetings, and . . . told to keep silent when NASA representatives were at the plant."[53] A resignation letter from Christina Ferrari, an employee in structures design, indicated severe safety problems at the Thiokol Wasatch plant. Engineer Steve Agee noted that before he left, he had written over 200 critical hazard reports, all of which were ignored by a Thiokol safety professional.[54] He also cited the "reckless use of waivers and deviations," normal processes to speed up production which were bought by the hundreds by NASA while he was there. "NASA . . . needed waivers and deviations like a drug addict needs his drugs."[55] A "Say no to waivers and deviations!" campaign might have been more beneficial, in retrospect, for the moral safety of America's schoolchildren than the current slogan.

Thiokol was even able to "successfully petition NASA to affect

formal closure of the O-ring problem"—that is, its elimination
from Marshall's monthly problems reports. The Thiokol request
was based on strange logic: tests leading to a safe redesign were
underway; therefore, the problem was being addressed; therefore,
it was no longer an open problem. "The incredible request worked.
... Only five days before the *Challenger* accident, a Marshall
message indicated that the 'problem is considered closed.' "[56]

Indeed, two others emerge as persons who questioned the
instrumental bureaucratic rationality of Thiokol safety decisions:
Thiokol engineer Roger Boisjoly and Arnold Thompson, supervisor
of Rocket Motor Cases. Thompson and Boisjoly argued vehe-
mently both through memoranda and at the infamous teleconference set up the evening before scheduled launch to discuss
concerns. These engineers argued in an hour-long presentation that
the seals would be in certain jeopardy should launch take place in
such cold temperatures as were predicted. The consensus testimony at the Roger's Commission Hearings is that Marshall's
director of the solid rocket booster project, Larry Mulloy's response
to their no-launch recommendation was unusually heated. "My
God, Thiokol," he argued, "when do you want me to launch, next
April?"[57] Indeed, the high-tech teleconference, which could have
resulted in a launch delay, was "far different from a neutral
assessment of data ... mutual deception lay at the heart of the
exchange between NASA and Morton-Thiokol. The men from
Marshall wanted their launch to proceed on schedule and would
listen to no reasonable argument that recommended delay. The
Thiokol managers overruled their engineering experts to satisfy a
demanding customer."[58]

The heart of bureaucratic rationality is revealed, in the moment
when Thompson and Boisjoly desperately reemphasized the crucial
nature of their recommendations, Thompson frantically drawing
mock-joint assemblies, Boisjoly "grabbing a pile of photographs
to show the serious erosion on flight 51-C."[59] At this point Jerald
Mason, senior vice-president of Thiokol's Wasatch operation asked
Bob Lund, Thiokol's vice-president of Engineering, to "*take off
your engineering hat and put on your management hat.*"[60] This

request clearly implies an epistemic switch from truths that can affect flight safety to "truths" which can affect company market position, with a demanding customer on the line. It is this instrumental switch that lies at the heart of the *Challenger* incident. There was simply nothing accidental about it. And we must be reminded that in return for a $10 million reduction in award fees, all charges against Thiokol were dropped, and not one of the managers who made the decision to launch was fired.[61]

AWAY FROM GOODNESS: A CONCLUSION

There is certainly a bitter irony in this fact, that in the heart of the so-called information age one can know so little of the truth about such an important and so public an event. What I am left with are the flashes of understanding amid a contradictory and frightening reality. I recall the multiple efforts to manage what was called "the grief" of the young after this event. As if mourning, and not anger, was the only possible emotion to feel. Arendt reminds us, "absence of emotions neither causes nor promotes rationality" and "detachment and equanimity [in view of] unbearable tragedy can indeed be terrifying, namely when they are not the result of control but an evident manifestation of incomprehension."[62]

During the 1980s we were led to believe the argument that our technique was failing and our productivity suffered as a result of the "rising tide of mediocrity." Ronald Reagan's White House statement to the ten *Challenger* teacher contest finalists rang with this theme ominously ironic not only for the disaster that would follow, but the propaganda that would teach us its meaning. "You save our past," he said, "from being consumed by forgetfulness and our future from being engulfed in ignorance, . . . when one of you blasts off from Cape Canaveral next January, you will represent hope and opportunity and possibility; you will be the emissary to the next generation of American heroes. And your message will be that our progress, impressive as it is, is only just a beginning; that our achievements, as great as they are, are only a launching pad into the future. Flying up above the atmosphere, you'll be able to truly say that our horizons are not our limits, only new frontiers to be explored."[63]

David Purpel cites Reinhold Niebuhr, who said, "educators, as well as other middle-class moralists, underestimate the conflict of interest in political and economic relations."[64] Education reform in the 1980s worked to further obscure this conflict by mystifying the meaning and potential of high technology to better lives across class categories. The core curriculum and revised standards of excellence, however, tend to eliminate efforts to distribute reflective, critical literacy across social and school classes. As Purpel notes, those redistributive efforts, which had some potential to be socially and politically significant—open admissions, politically and socially "relevant" studies, multicultural studies, preschool and compensatory education—have all come under some form of attack from conservative school reforms.[65] Despite the rhetoric of excellence, the "new basics" of education reform emphasizes intensified traditional curriculum with meritocratic presuppositions likely to prevent all students from participating in reflective thinking and awareness. Excellence mediates social conflict by redefining pedagogy in service of technical, not civic, competence. The democratic potential, the emancipatory power of reflection is muted in the intoxication of space spectacle, automation, computerspeak, and high-class education as a sort of pledge period best endured by those students who already know the rules of the fraternity.

Shapiro discusses the recommendations of the National Commission on Excellence in Education (NCEE) that argued for intensified state intervention to increase the productivity of education. He also discusses the National Task Force on Education for Economic Growth (NTFEEG) that refined this call by focusing rhetoric around the demands of competition. Whatever arguments there are for citizenship education and civic literacy are muted by the demand for results in the marketplace. In the same way the ethical purposes of democratic life are twisted in the service of bureaucrats and production quotas. Civic life eschews reflection on the ends of production by an intoxication with means.[66] Central to the 1980s reform effort was a conservative effort to "control cultural symbols and meanings . . . given the overwhelming power of corporate interests to manufacture and manipulate culture."[67] One cannot help but note the way the *Challenger* is a graphic example of the management of illusion and spectacle characterizing an important link in the cynical reform agenda. We would be left with a different story in a nation that took seriously the nature of its real risks and the way education can help.

The national memory that did justice to Christa McAuliffe would remind us of the intensity of her insistence that she maintain control over her participation. We only see glimmers of this, however. We are reminded how despite the fact that NASA's excellent public relations department, who could have provided her class with reams of material to teach from while she was competing for the shuttle spot, she refused to rely on them.[68] This, plus her fight to overrule the script developed for her are an emblem of the person and the teacher she must have been.

One of the truly enormous ironies of the intersection of the shuttle disaster, the high-tech computer revolution, and education is noted by Richard Feynman, who was a member of the Rogers Commission that investigated the shuttle disaster. He describes the simple fact that nobody needs to be on the shuttle to fly it. The entire flight was controlled by computers programmed on the ground. The shuttle gets into orbit automatically. The shuttle descends and lands automatically. The only thing required of the astronauts is that after the shuttle gets into flight, they load the programs for the next phase of flight, because the computer does not have enough memory. Then they load for descent and landing. It even brakes automatically after landing. An odd remnant of control is kept, however. The astronauts push the button for the landing gear to come down at around 4,000 feet. There is no particular reason for this. Feynman argues it remains, despite the danger that the passengers might be unconscious or incapacitated in some way, because the astronauts or their promoters cannot stand the idea that they have nothing to do. If the computers were

more up-to-date, at least in 1986, the passengers (pilots?) would
not be required to load memory either.[69]

This simulation of control is oddly apropos for the central
message of the high-tech, computer revolution, where the illusion
of worker control is necessary only in some sectors of labor, where
automation threatens the symbolism of human autonomy, where
that autonomy is required for ideological legitimation more centralized control of production.

I remember reflecting with vague unease that I would have to
step on a jetliner to get to Florida for the delivery of the paper which
formed an early draft of this chapter, not far from where the
Challenger sat on its last launch site. I remember waiting, at times
edgily, anticipating the air travel I have never relished. It was at
this point that Christa McAuliffe's courage to place herself in
the nose of a space shuttle became palpable. Note a passage from
McConnell: "Throughout the banter that morning, Judy Resnik
and Ellison Onizuka had been the most jocular. . . . Onizuka rolled
to his left (to get a look at the liquid oxygen vent arm retract).
'Doesn't it go the other way?' he quipped. A flight test engineer
with more than a thousand hours in advanced aircraft, Ellison was
famous for his irreverent attitude toward high-tech hardware. . . .
'There goes the beanie cap,' said Scobee. . . . Since the first
communication checks two hours earlier, Christa McAuliffe had
been silent." Silent. I have to conclude that McAuliffe, by her
inexperience, was, as any civilian would be, fighting fear.[70]

However, in addition, Richard Feynman, the Nobel Laureate
who served as an investigator on the Rogers Commission investi-
gating the disaster, wrote that during her association with the other
astronauts McAuliffe had learned a great deal about the risks of
shuttle flight. You did not have to be a "rocket scientist" to figure
those out. These risks, which were significant, were the kind of
which the general public was never made fully aware. Yet even
these did not include the unnecessary risk brought about by slipping
safety criteria and managements' squelching engineers' warnings
of impending disaster.[71]

After eight years I am still awed by her enormous courage; more

courage, because of her inexperience, than any other of her crew-
mates, who were no slouches in that department either. In those
things, it seems to me, lay the proper honor of her memory. She
should not continue in posterity to serve as a propaganda surrogate.
Her story and the story of the *Challenger* disaster speak clearly of
that which is truly at risk in America today. The disaster was caused
by the fear and duplicity of managers with more than enough math
and science education to design a safe field joint, but not the kind
of education that enables one to summon the guts or insight to
separate launch pressures from the real dangers present on the
launch pad that frigid day. It is perhaps for the same reason that
the true quality of American life has declined in more ways than
can be linked to Japanese industrial competition. There was certainly a rising tide of something. After a careful study of this event
and its meaning for education, mediocrity is not the word which
comes first to mind.

Her real risk, the one that might really teach us something, has
been obscured—that it was not engineering skill but ethics that
were lacking and caused the real danger. We may reflect that her
high achievement as a social studies teacher was put aside in favor
of her "girl-next-door" wholesomeness, picked despite having the
"weakest" résumé. Perhaps judges felt that her intellect would not
as likely get in the way of her readily acquiescing to the script. If
that is true, they were wrong. If truth would be told about the value
of the shuttle lesson, it would be in her courage and her firm
resistance, despite her résumé, to the script and the public relations
hyperbole. The legitimate story would be that America is not at
risk because it lacks engineering and high-tech skill, but because
it has a shortage of an education that shapes engineers like Roger
Boisjoly, Christina Ferrari, and Arnold Thompson, and an excess
of an education and a bureaucratic culture that builds and rewards
a Larry Mulloy, a William Lucas.

It would be, and painfully remains Christa McAuliffe's job to
boost education reform in the service of the high-tech revolution.
For a society that has reified commodity values by propaganda,
bureaucracy, and the attendant violence of state information

monopolies, it was Christa McAuliffe's job to de-mystify space for ordinary Americans. In America, space is not the mystery.

NOTES

1. David Friend, "Seeing Beyond the Stars," *Life* (December 1985): 29–41, 36.
2. *Report of the Presidential Commission on the Space Shuttle Challenger Accident* (Washington, D.C.: GPO, 1986), p. 89.
3. Sun Ra is a musician who realized the purpose of space a number of years ago.
4. Douglas Kellner, *Critical Theory, Marxism, and Modernity* (Baltimore: Johns Hopkins University Press, 1989).
5. See Hannah Arendt, *On Violence* (New York: Harcourt Brace, 1970). Also, Jacques Ellul, *Propaganda: The Formation of Men's Attitudes* (New York: Alfred A. Knopf, 1965).
6. Kellner, *Critical Theory*, p. 232. See Douglas Kellner, *Jean Baudrillard: From Marxism to Postmodernism and Beyond* (Stanford, Calif.: Stanford University Press, 1989). Baudrillard's discussion of simulation and the surrogate in social presentation is a particularly useful adjunct to Ellul. See also Franklin Rosemont, *André Breton: What Is Surrealism?* (New York: Monad, 1978). Surrealism provides the impetus for us to take chance juxtapositions and symbolic occurrences for their intellectually liberatory potential. With this encouragement the *Challenger* narrative becomes potent as social metaphor.
7. *New York Times Magazine* (January 5, 1986): 19.
8. Hal Quinn with Sharon Doyle, "A Space Tragedy," *Maclean's Magazine* (February 10, 1986): 26.
9. Ibid.
10. Ibid.
11. Robert T. Hohler, *"I Touch the Future . . .": The Story of Christa McAuliffe* (New York: Random House, 1986), p. 72.
12. Ibid., p. 141.
13. Ibid.
14. Ibid.
15. Ibid., p. 170.
16. Ibid., p. 171.
17. Ibid.
18. See Richard Wightman Fox and T. J. Jackson Lears, *The Culture of Consumption: Critical Essays in American History, 1880–1980* (New York: Pantheon, 1983), pp. 177–209.
19. Ibid., p. 183.
20. Ibid., pp. 184–185.

21. Richard Brosio, *The Frankfurt School: An Analysis of the Contradictions and Crises of Liberal Capitalist Societies*, Ball State University Monograph 29 (1980), p. 17.

22. Martin Carnoy, "High Technology and Education: An Economist's View," in Steven Tozer and Kenneth D. Benne, eds., *Society as Educator in an Age of Transition*, National Society for the Study of Education (Chicago: University of Chicago Press, 1987).

23. Christine M. Shea, "Pentagon vs. Multinational Capitalism: The Political Economy of the 1980's School Reform Movement," in Christine M. Shea, Ernest Kahane, and Peter Sola, eds., *The New Servants of Power: A Critique of the 1980's School Reform Movement* (New York: Praeger, 1990), p. 19.

24. Hohler, *I Touch the Future*, p. 252.

25. Jacques Ellul, *Propaganda: The Formation of Men's Attitudes* (New York: Alfred A. Knopf, 1965).

26. Ibid, pp. 121–122.

27. *Chicago Tribune* (January 29, 1986): 6.

28. Ibid.

29. Malcolm McConnell, *Challenger: A Major Malfunction* (Garden City, N.Y.: Doubleday, 1987), p. 83.

30. Ibid.

31. Ibid., p. 147.

32. McConnell, *Challenger*, pp. 118–19.

33. Ibid., p. 119.

34. Ellul, *Propaganda*, p. 165.

35. Ibid., p. 55.

36. McConnell, *Challenger*, p. 22.

37. Ibid., p. 23.

38. Ellul, *Propaganda*, p. 106.

39. Ibid., p. 148.

40. Frederic Jameson, *Marxism and Form* (Princeton: Princeton University Press, 1971).

41. Franklin Rosemont, *André Breton: What Is Surrealism?* (New York: Monad, 1978), p. 71.

42. *Aviation Week and Space Technology* (January 26, 1987): 13.

43. Ibid.

44. Arendt, *On Violence*, p. 38.

45. Ibid., p. 46.

46. Charles Peters, "From Ouagadougou to Cape Canaveral: Why the Bad News Doesn't Travel Up," *The Washington Monthly* (April, 1986): pp. 27–31, 28.

47. Ibid.

48. Ibid.

49. Ibid.

50. Ibid.

51. Ibid., p. 46.

52. "Two Minutes." *Financial World* (June 27, 1989): 28–32, 29.

53. Ibid.

54. Ibid., p. 30.

55. Ibid.

56. McConnell, *Challenger*, p. 181.

57. Ibid., p. 196.

58. Ibid., p. 203.

59. Ibid., p. 199.

60. Ibid.

61. Ibid., p. 32.

62. Arendt, *On Violence*, p. 64.

63. Hohler, *I Touch the Future*, p. 89.

64. David Purpel, *The Moral and Spiritual Crisis in Education: A Curriculum for Justice and Compassion in Education* (New York: Bergin & Garvey, 1989), p. 14.

65. Ibid., p. 15.

66. Svi Shapiro, *Between Capitalism and Democracy: Educational Policy and the Crisis of the Welfare State* (New York: Bergin & Garvey, 1990), p. 130.

67. Ibid., p. 152.

68. Peggy Lathlaen, "The Town that Remembers Christa," *Ladies Home Journal*, p. 150.

69. McConnell, *Challenger*, p. 238. Also, Richard P. Feynman, *What Do You Care What Other People Think?* (New York: Bantam Books, 1988), p. 191. Part 2 of this book is an important contribution to an understanding of the politics of a federal investigation of this sort.

70. McConnell, *Challenger*, p. 238.

71. Feynman, *What Do You Care?*, p. 181.

3

KO in Twelve: Boxing, Schooling, and Rackets as Theory and Metaphor

This chapter reflects the harsh light of scrutiny from our nation's most powerfully metaphoric and transparent enterprise, to illuminate its ambiguous counterpart, an enterprise that carries the hopes of succeeding generations in its struggles. It leaves the reader to decide the direction of the light. It is an effort frankly to obscure the difference between boxing and schooling, in order to provide evidence that both are intended to be enjoyed uncritically, fruits of a harsh climate. This essay will compare boxing and education reform. This is the aesthetic deliquescence of categories of apparent opposites, and the actual deliquescence of youth in the assaults of violent competition.

The following list of questions is an example of this: What is more money for education? What is a racket? What are gaming revenues? What is sacrifice, upward mobility, martyrdom, public relations? What is a "tomato can"? An opponent? What is brain damage? Accidental death? A promoter, a lie? Who is José Torres, and what does he mean when he says, "We fighters understand lies."[1] What's a feint? What's a left hook off the jab? What's an opening? What's thinking one thing and doing another. What does the fighter's saying "Kill the Body and the Head Dies" mean in a different arena? What is exploitation obscured by glamor? This chapter will argue by its presentation that the struggle to reform in boxing and schooling during the 1980s is overshadowed by the socialization and legitimation of failure, however obscured and formalized for control of the illusion of fair struggle. Indeed, victory is formalized. Reform's object has obscured any possible sense of public injustice by controlling and valorizing a discourse of ritual struggle. This chapter will argue that only when human agency is mediated by reform can human sacrifices attendant to the actual struggles occurring beneath the spectacle be justified. Violence becomes rehabilitation for the next occasion of violence.

It is perhaps only coincidental that the last great push for reform in both boxing and schooling occurred in the early 1980s. The trajectories of these two reform impulses intersect in discomfiting ways, symbols and areas of intervention, methods of control, even exemplars and martyrs in each impulse eerily cohabit the same discourse. Deuk Koo Kim, who writes on a lampshade the night before the fight in which he dies "Kill or Be Killed" becomes a martyr and part of the 1980s reform impulse. Christa McAuliffe who says, "if the teacher in space doesn't come back to teach, something's wrong" serves a myth as she is destroyed by a host of misleading and miseducational factors. Both individuals, real lives lost, become centerpieces in a reform impulse.

In the 1980s, New Jersey emerged as the state instituting radical education and boxing reform proposals. Both enterprises were seen as a precious engine of economic growth. Out of these proposals arises a symbiosis of metaphors for struggle and rehabilitative competition which, I will argue, lie at the heart of the persistent ability of education and boxing to blend: both as enterprises that specialize in seeming to be something they are not, standing for things which they are not about. This analysis draws on a number of theoretical insights but will focus on the development of simulation in social life which Baudrillard develops, and upon Horkheimer's theory of "rackets": where institutions serve to protect as they exploit.

The result is a sort of toboggan ride through a forest of signifiers, rather than a linear argument with a series of connected premises and a conclusion. This is an effort to interpret the fluctuation of power in the reform efforts at hand, by what Jameson calls "punctual demystification, de-idealization, involving a certain shock, a painful rebuke to our own habits of idealization."[2] To paraphrase Lautréamont's proto-surrealist epigram, it is the fortuitous meeting of a boxer and a pupil on an operating table.

BRAIN INJURY

Both efforts at reform, in schooling and boxing, are discussions of the brain, about what prevents it from functioning, about knockouts and ignorance, comas and illiteracy. Prize rings and schools are both full of bells. Bells for stopping and starting, time frames for potential. Both are run by managers, and pushed by promoters who do not get hurt. The rounds, limited and arbitrary, like grade levels, are carefully timed for the appearance of students/ boxers being fairly matched at the start. Both enterprises, because they affect one for life, take from individuals enormous amounts of time and do something to their brains. Both activities are arenas of attraction and repulsion to which the sensitive heads of the nation pay ambiguous heed. Indeed, the reform efforts of the early 1980s were centered on the problem of brain damage, but if you examine the discourse of reform in boxing you can see it is not the damage of brains that becomes the center of concern, rather it is the appearance of unfairness in the distribution of damage. It is the lack of management being present when the damage occurs. Likewise in schooling, the tocsin of excellence, preventing the greater effects of mass stupefaction, reveals a basic disregard of the deratiocination required in much of the central arguments. Also revealing how the reforms, leading to a better education for productivity gains manifest a numb disregard for the deeper depredations of struggle in an increasingly untenable working-class position in the postindustrial markets in labor.

Much of the effort to reform boxing developed in the early 1980s through a discourse fraught with references to desired standards of fairness. Reformers were concerned with increased involvement of organized crime, payoffs, thrown fights, and so on, but even more were concerned with the persistent cries of permanent brain damage suffered by professional and amateur alike, along with the occasional "accidental" ring death. Max Novich, of the Association of Ringside Physicians, testified before Congress in 1983 at hearings regarding the "Federal Boxing Protection Act." Novich argued that the "glaring fault" of professional boxing and the ring deaths under scrutiny are the result of "administrative mistakes." Referring to the death of Kim in New Jersey, he decried the lack of a standard examination for the licensing of boxers.[3] This standardization of examination supplants any fear that boxers will be injured, that brains will be hurt, or that ring deaths will be a concern.

Opponents of boxing have long dealt with a litany of arguments regarding the character-training benefits of the sport: the "strict discipline, tolerance to pain, resolution, alertness, courage, and endurance."[4] Testimony in the reform hearings of the 1980s shows an effort to save the sport by appeal that these qualities along with the ability to control its damaging aspects by attention to scrupulous bureaucratic administrative methods. "Boxing is worth saving, as you must realize that the sport has saved many lives, in both the contestants and victims, by taking many youngsters off the streets and making disciplined young men out of them."[5]

During one set of hearings Bert Sugar, editor of the popular journal *The Ring* entered the argument with fierce criticism of the prevailing organizational structures governing the sport, particularly the World Boxing Association (WBA). His testimony responded directly to the death of Deuk Koo Kim, the Korean fighter killed in the ring by Ray Mancini. His comments are sensitive to the negative educational impact of a fight, which because of the ubiquity of media, became a focus of national discussion. His concern is with Kim's lack of preparation for the fight, the sense that the WBA sent up another "stiff."[6] Sugar says that "A KO is not a KO is not a KO, to misquote G. Stein" and "if you are knocked out, Congressman, it might be a cut eye and it might be five days later you could fight again . . . if I am knocked out, knowing my luck, I would be comatose for twenty minutes. That is different, and that must show up on a piece of computer hardware in every office instantaneously."[7]

These excerpts point to a particularly important fact. The underlying presence of brain assault and damage is not questioned here. But there is a sense developing that if one could institute a standardized procedure for measuring boxers by a set of criteria, and process that information through a centralized information clearinghouse, boxing would be reformed in a meaningful way.

It is not unimportant that the reform movement in education at the same time also reflects an impulse to create more rigorously applied state-administered assessments in order to regularize and make effective the resultant schooling competition for useful knowledge. This is allied to the impulse for accumulating information in databases which encourage efficiency, but which likewise ignore the underlying struggle of working-class children whose intensified competition in the classroom is only tangentially related to later prospects in the postindustrial workforce. This struggle takes on the painful character of violence in schools with metal detectors and the surveillance tactics of the penitentiary. Indeed, with old warrior Jersey Joe Walcott presiding on that state's athletic commission, it is not merely coincidental that the pedagogic heroes of the Reagan years followed not the dream of King, but the bat of "Jersey" Joe Clark.[8] There is an undercurrent of violent conflict within school walls with forces of degeneracy developing from without. This chapter attempts a straightforward approach to dealing with a host of schooling problems, linear, a straight right.

NEW JERSEY EDUCATION REFORM

New Jersey would reform its teachers in a somewhat different fashion than it did its fighters. By September 1985 local districts would be able to offer the first district-administered training programs in the United States leading to teacher certification. Oddly this system was to replace a system where "emergency certification would staff up to 20 percent of all newly employed New Jersey teachers entering the system. It is the replacement of out-of-control maverick certification with in-control maverick certification. It is the control that counts.[9]

New Jersey's *Boyer Report* on the preparation of beginning teachers attacked low standards not by decentralizing but by replacing one locus of control, state and university teacher certification, with competing, also state-approved, district training programs. Yet it is a promotional change with low-level goals, to identify the basic knowledge and skills essential for all beginning teachers, Governor Thomas Kean appointed a panel of ten distinguished leaders headed by Ernest Boyer. The mission of this group was to determine what things beginning teachers must know and how effective teachers teach. Teachers must know (1) the curriculum priorities of the school; (2) how to assess student progress; how to organize instruction; (3) how to develop and use evaluations; (4) how students learn, alone and in groups; (5) how to motivate students; (6) how to maintain a healthy classroom climate; and (7) how the classroom and the school function as social units.[10]

In short, teachers are to be reformed as stiffs, low-level functional thinkers with no required awareness of their professional commitment outside the confines of the district rules. The lowering of living standards and the reduction of bargaining power due to the increased supply of instructors is not mentioned, but also supposedly redounds to the benefit of the district.[11]

Reform efforts in both spheres appear to be chiefly locus-of-control battles. While these disputes unfold, the flaws inherent in both areas become further obscured by the distraction of attention away from those flaws. Reform becomes moralizing as distraction (from violence, from the corrosions of worker displacement, and increasing poverty).

Turning to the boxing reform discussion in New Jersey, Bershad and Ensor outline a debate that occurs entirely within a context of locus-of-control, ignoring the physical exploitation of boxers in the state. They discuss the "effort to make boxing safer and more reputable within the state."[12] They cite how, "in recent times especially during the 1980s, boxing sustained attacks in two areas . . . first for the manner in which it crowns champions and ranks boxers, and from "external criticism, because of its brutality and inherent health risks, as well as its alleged links to organized crime."[13] Yet despite the internal and external debate, all debate will function within the reform context as subsidiary to the economic value of the enterprise.

A New Jersey consumer affairs director stated that boxing is one of only a few industries in the nation which have grown by more than 100 percent in one year—1983. New Jersey Governor Kean (who was simultaneously presiding over the education reforms) stated that while "economic factors alone cannot take precedence over safety and medical concerns, New Jersey *has* become the boxing capital of the nation."[14] Kean maintains a position that to salvage this activity, the state must be committed to improving the *safety of boxing* within the state. One of the arguments for increasing safety moves from paradox to black humor when we read "Advanced life support systems must be available at ringside."[15] Some might argue "if boxing is a sport, it is the most tragic of sports," while others who wish simply to abolish boxing are ignored.[16] They are dismissed "as to a ban on boxing in the state. New Jersey officials have wisely ignored those recommendations."[17] Due to the importance (of the sport) to the state's economy New Jersey must continue its efforts to reform the sport.[18] In the meantime while New Jersey "has set a standard for the rest of the nation to follow in its regulation of boxing,"[19] it engages unprecedented effort to deregulate schooling.

The uneasy opposition of boxing and schooling comes together in an article by Steven Heyman, where he considers the knotty ethical problem of teaching boxers to hurt each other. He discusses the central conundrum where "whether at the amateur level or the professional level, freak accidents and congenital weaknesses aside, repeated blows to the head seem likely to cause brain damage. Thus an amateur who has had 150 or 250 matches, no matter how well regulated each is, can sustain gradually increasing cortical damage."[20] Heyman muses, "Will working on performance enhancement help this individual to get into a situation in which he or she might be hurt?"[21] Underlying this definition of boxing is acceptance of brain destruction. Thus in victory, defeat also occurs. This problem is embodied in the activity itself, which under current conditions is past reform. Michele Fine, in a recent article, meditates on a decade of "hopeless narratives on public education." She is concerned about the two "big-education images" both bankrupt: (1) privatized, market-driven education and (2) public-sector education. Her "worry is about the national move to write/Right off poor urban students, embodied in the growing pressure to privatize public schooling. Second, [she is] concerned that the texts of education . . . over the past decade constitute a problematic raft of hopeless narratives." We must not, she argues, "lose the moment. We must resuscitate, quickly and collectively, narrative images of public education in which critical democratic inquiry can flourish for children."[22]

Resuscitating images may cheer up discouraged educational theorists, but this discourse is a reminder of how much activity on any level, theoretical or practical, depends on the maintenance of democratic, rational simulations for the conduct of any school business. It is the same in schooling and in boxing, the maintenance of an ongoing activity that deprives thousands of its participants of a healthy cerebrum.

Boxers and working-class students are both involved in a simulation of mortal combat for life chances, but the real struggle for insight into the workings that really put their future at risk are kept obscure by both reactionaries and their foes, the reformers. It is here that the theoretical work of Baudrillard, the illusionist, and Horkheimer, the Elliot Ness of critical theory, may come together.

BAUDRILLARD

For Baudrillard, reform projects can be understood as quasi-public advertisements and promotions. These promotions enter the world of consumer circulation independent of the logic of capital accumulation.[23] The power of this circulation is a function of ideology only tangentially related to the facticity of the object of the promotion. For boxing, the damaging, sometimes death-dealing struggle is obscured when reformers shape the debate. This shaping works to alter the true dangers of the activity and serves as advertisements for the importance of reformers. For education, the ideology of equal opportunity and excellence is an advertisement for the deeper struggle where public-school compulsion becomes the standardized substitute for the lost power of working-class persons to amass private goods and time for their own and their communities' betterment. The orchestration of schooling appears in this light somewhat like a dance marathon, a decorous and energetic activity initially, but one which grinds to an obscure and deadly march of endurance and success of a few only at the expense of those contestants who fall. We may follow Baudrillard into his world, where what things *stand for* are more important than what they *are for*. Reform, as a sort of spectacular, decorous democratic mobilization of care, stands for rectitude, but is coded to promote little if any substantial change. Indeed Baudrillard claimed that "control of the code" and the proliferation of sign values are of more significance than control of labor and the sphere of production.[24] He argued for theoretical perspective in which the most fruitful area of approach is to oppose and expose the process of signification that makes possible the process of obscurity, which operates as a function of the symbolic universe of competition and struggle in capitalist societies. For Baudrillard, capital itself is a "demented enterprise, without limits, to abolish the symbolic universe in an indifference that is always greater, and in circulation of values always accelerated . . . capital is described as the reign without limits of exchange value."[25] Thus the de-mentation of participants in a competitive struggle must be met by the de-mentation of our efforts to describe and define the symbolic universe encapsulating these struggles. Boxing and schooling play a part in this symbolic universe, and all efforts to reform must also reform their metaphorical message. For Baudrillard the struggles of Right and Left, which have their counterpart in reform efforts in education, particularly have imploded in a media-saturated society, in which differences become signs simulating democratic debate.[26] Capital is itself a fundamental challenge to the natural order of value and moral hierarchy. Justice and reason are only accidental to its efficiencies.

With Baudrillard we might argue that reform and democratic process "involve the injection of homeopathic doses of the social and the political into a body in which the previous vestiges are dying."[27]

COMPETITIVE EXCELLENCE

Svi Shapiro contributed an analysis of the 1980s excellence movement that illuminates some of these homeopathic and spectacular elements of education reform. He argued, for example, that the National Commission on Excellence in Education (NCEE) report, "while stopping short of calling for new outlays, also makes clear its support for a strong federal role."[28] This highlights the paradoxical allegiance to a "new federalism," evident in the growing privatization impulse, while the education of children is quietly redefined as the sole protectorate of a "*national* interest." This interest is that of business primarily, and the NCEE report's apparent concern with education in the humanities, civics, or the development of a "literate citizenry" are in fact subsidiary to the human capital development interests of business. "Knowledge, learning information and skilled intelligence are the new raw materials of international commerce," the report concludes, "and are today spreading throughout the world as vigorously as miracle drugs . . . if only to keep and improve on the slim competitive edge we will retain in world markets, we must rededicate ourselves to the reform of our educational system."[29] Yet, disguised by the metaphors of expansion and productivity is the reality for working-class children of the struggle for what they hope are actual, not symbolic, life chances. Yet, while that increased productivity may come from technological innovation and may more likely be derived from a process of "reforming" the existing work process to their disadvantage, through automation, layoffs, out-sourcing, speedups, replacement of full-time employees with temporaries, benefits reductions, and capital relocation.

For example, computers hold the honored place as the mechanical warrior at the barricades of the high-tech revolution. Their benefits and wonders occupy our attention as a part of the post-industrial spectacle. Ironically, they are the apogee of the marriage of mind and machine which is at the heart of education reform intoxication with math and science and engineering applications. Computers appear to offer an opportunity to increase and diversify the level of interest and complexity in curriculum to correspond to their complexity. In addition, as Kahane and Oram argue, "computers symbolize egalitarianism, sharing, openness to change, constant growth and advancement and a quest for excellence."[30]

There is increasing evidence, however, that much computer use by potential employees argues not for the education of excellent minds in control of a complex syntactic and communication environment. Rather, much new "computerization fits the traditional model of automation, whereby workers' discretion is lessened or displaced."[31] We are not becoming a society of programmers and systems analysts. "Other than a small layer of specialists in systems work, computers for the most part generated a huge supply of low-paying unskilled jobs, often occupied by temporary female labor."[32]

Peter Sola, quotes Harold Laski, noting the crucial nature of symbol organization for the smooth operation of capital, "The businessman dominates American civilization. His function is so to organize American society that he has the freest possible run of profitable adventure. To do this he must organize the symbolism of that society so that there are no vital obstacles to the performance of his function."[33] In a crucial way the violence of school competition is socialized by a faith that competition and struggle are fair. Yet we cannot ignore the enormity of failure which inhabits the lower recesses of shake-outs in the capitalist business cycle, or the attendant violence in our associated civil environments as expressions of frustrated and deflected working-class ambitions and desires. Richard Altenbaugh reflects on the climate of violence in schools when he reminds us of the enormous level of perceptions of personal danger held by New York City teachers, that, according to Boyer, "one-third of these teachers had been assaulted and that 40 percent reported their ongoing anxiety about the threat of violence."[34] Yet he correctly uses this reality to point out the deeper significance of violence in this society, where processes of segmentation and isolation have, in many cases, become part of our collective consciousness, an unstated assumption in any kind of activity. Here the depredations of decreasing life chance wrought by the postindustrial landscape appear as the fertile soil for alienation, frustration and normless aggression.[35]

Interestingly, José Torres, former light heavyweight champion, in an article for the *Washington Post* magazine, contemplated a "national curriculum, that deals with the understanding of fear and violence, to be taught in our schools."[36] Torres, who made his living with controlled application of punishment against struggling working-class fighters like himself, is concerned with the way street life engenders fear and violence. For him, the way to change the climate of gang warfare is to establish an "awareness" curriculum. Again we see a subtle marriage of two symbolic worlds. Schooling as a way to render rational the seeming irrational force within, the same force that makes boxing possible, the same "controlled fear" that Torres was taught separated the champions from the contenders. Just beyond Torres's grasp is a unified world where both actual violence and its symbolic representation are functional toward the end of legitimating widespread defeat in the working-class struggle for fair life chances.

Boxing, where reformers work toward the impression of fairness, still remains typically the struggle of two working-class men, one trying to destroy the other, destroying both brains in the process. Their struggle provides a spectacle of competition, and fuel for the establishment of symbolic upward social mobility. Yet the mobility of two men, selected by the fight game cartels that promote bouts, stands in truth at the top of a pyramid of bodies-club fighters, "stiffs," "tomato cans," "opponents" whose chief job is to lose for peanuts. Charles Leerhsen writes about the controversial Julio Chavez versus Pernell Whittaker title fight of mid 1993, and his observation takes on new meaning with this in mind. He writes describing both Whittaker's and Chavez's ascent from the streets to contender and champion status, telling in detail the urban wasteland of Culiacan, Mexico, run by dueling drug lords, a frenetic, if dirty and hopeless place, from which Chavez emerges. He writes, "Chavez treats opponents the way the world treats most young men who drift into the ring: he limits their opportunities."[37] This metaphor of working-class isolation, two men literally at each other's throats, a spectacle in the streets where drive-by shooting has become standard fare for middle-class clucking and "info-tainment," a spectacle in the ring.

REFINING THE BRAIN DEATH RACKET

Peter Stirk outlines Max Horkheimer's important, if undeveloped, theory of rackets, and in so doing provides a crucial explanation for the discipline of violence and corrosive competition. For Horkheimer, the archetypal form of domination was "protection" and that domination takes place within narrower confines than broad categories of class and strata.[38] What characterize rackets is the "ambiguous mixture conjured up in the term 'protection' which Horkheimer took as the archetype of domination. It signifies on the one hand protection from harm or disturbance. On the other hand, it signifies the extraction of tribute under threat of coercion. The racketeer is both protector and exploiter . . . in broader terms Horkheimer presented the racketeers as competing for a share in the circulating surplus value."[39]

It is within paradoxes such as these that reform in its common form, as a *reform within competing rackets* may be understood. Indeed, the notion of rackets is shot through the mythology of boxing in this century. The New Jersey State Commission of Investigation (SCI) reads in places like a pulp novel narrative: "despite memory lapses that seemed to occur only when interrogation touched on organized crime, and despite a posture of childlike innocence, the testimony of hard-bitten promoters, etc. corroborated the penetration of boxing in this state by mobsters."[40] Images of mugs nervously fingering their boutonnieres, darting their eyes to avoid eye contact with steely state interrogators making for an imaginative picture of moral rectitude exposing the criminality of the racket. In reality this scrutiny spectacle is a way to legitimize the anarchy of violence and deprivation called boxing-competing rackets, vying for the ability to offer protection to the fighter while exploiting his eventual neural destruction for profit. The bureaucratic rationalization of violence, how "without legislative intervention to formulate uniform health, safety, labor, and statistical standards, the problem of the boxing industry will continue."[41] Reform becomes a way to rationalize the physical and financial destruction of fighters.

Dominant classes, for Horkheimer, are a structure of rackets based on a definite mode of production, holding down and "protecting" lower orders.[42] Rackets emerge as reformers in this analysis in that they claim to occupy a practical and moral high ground regarding the refinement or perfection of symbolic institutions, here boxing and schooling. A racket means having privileges within national boundaries, including the ongoing protective/exploitative relationship of reformer to the object of reform. For Horkheimer, the historical progress of the proletariat had led to a crossroads: it could become a class or a racket. Becoming a class meant world revolution.[43] "The American example was prominent when Horkheimer asserted that there was a similarity between labor organizations and the cartels of large capital. . . . bourgeois history was heavily oriented to a model composed of competitive individuals on the one hand and the anarchic outcome of the social process on the other." Anarchy stands as an "affront to the aspiration towards man's rational control of his own fate as espoused by bourgeois philosophers."[44]

The corrosive competition, alienation, and attendant violence of the aforementioned objects of reform, boxing and schooling, reaffirm the metaphoric presentation of fair struggle as a replacement for the unfair "competition" which passes for experience in both these arenas. "In the model of bourgeois society the fate of the individual was uncertain because the market-based operation of that society was opaque."[45] Just as opaque is the relation between world and national human capital development which ignores humane purpose in the means of production and corresponds with schooling that only superficially conforms to the requirements of decent intellectual development. The society of rackets entailed an "even more violent disregard of the individual by the arbitrary division of men into participants in the rackets and their victims. . . . competition and outright conflict was endemic."[46]

   For Horkheimer, through the function of symbolism, the manipulatory techniques have graduated to this period from earlier periods of bourgeois history. They have moved to an area beyond persuasion. In this era the general intent is "radically to alter the individual's perception of himself. It is to bring men to be filled with a sense not of their own person, but of the nullity of their person . . . in the modern era the intent and need was to remold the very characters of free men in order to adapt them to the exigencies for the new social system."[47]

   Institutions are seen here as systems of protection and exploitation, and in keeping with self-preservatory manipulation, advertisements for themselves. Freire maintains that "a particular cultural epoch is premised upon a 'thematic universe' which defines the consciousness of the people in that historical moment. The fundamental theme of our present epoch is domination."[48] He argues that extractive power relation is a dual consciousness that contains "both the sense of oppression and image of the oppressor within."[49] We might ask what the role of reformers is in the development of dominance systems. Or we might concentrate more on the role of the manager, the promoter as integral to the development of the institutional protection and exploitation in both boxing and schooling.

   In 1985 hearings in the House of Representatives were held on a bill with the wonderfully ironic title, "bill to promote health and safety in professional boxing." Thus in a sport where 80 to 90 percent of regular participants suffer measurable brain damage, Representative Richardson can say, "The health and safety of boxers should be our number one concern."[50] Perhaps it should be, but it remains an effort to install federal jurisdiction with a panel of presidentially appointed boardmembers of "The American Boxing Corporation" to oversee but not to supplant "legitimate boxing organizations."[51] This appears to be a racket supporting and overseeing appropriate subrackets in the guise of reform. It is as if a national registry of weights, experience, and "a rating of such boxers according to relative boxing abilities" will undo the fundamental change taking place at the root of the sport—permanent brain damage.[52] Yet persistent testimony is presented documenting the healthful character-building effects of the sport on minority and poor youth, kids whose access to their own healthy brain tissue would seem crucial in any meaningful struggle against tough odds for life chances in or out of school.

Indeed, the hearings include the testimony of Dr. George Lundberg, a persistent voice for abolition. He discusses the irony of the argument that brain damage should be coincident with upward mobility. And he protests that no form of data retrieval, no standardization process, no oversight can change the fact the simple act of boxing causes a high percentage of boxers to suffer some level of permanent brain damage. "No reliable test exists to identify in advance those boxers who will be subject to sudden death or brain injury."[53] He continues, "while it us undeniable that boxing has provided a way out of poverty for a relatively few participants, even for that handful of boxers the price they pay in terms of chronic brain damage and other adverse health effects may be high . . . the fact remains, that for the overwhelming majority of boxers, the promise of fame and fortune is illusory. For every Muhammad Ali, there are countless other boxers who not only may similarly suffer adverse health effects, but will (unlike Ali) receive little or nothing in terms of financial reward."[54]

"SAVE ME, JOE LOUIS"

Gerald Early writes that "boxing as an official bureaucracy hates boxers."[55] Early refers to his memory of the night he could not sleep after watching Benny Paret killed in the ring by Emile Griffith in the welterweight championship fight of March 1962. This is the same bureaucracy responsible for the "parade" of stiffs who routinely give their health as tribute on the altar of the sport. Early opines that professional prizefighting cannot be reformed, that its fighters are seen as so much meat whose work is more pointless than any imagined production work, but with the attached illusion of the self-reliant struggling individual central to the American myth. Early suggests the proletarian mythology of the competitors in a gladiator's struggle with so few winners. Proletariat is the appropriate word for fighters we call stiffs and bums. Stiff, as in working stiff, is someone who manages to survive in the working world, if working is a job like death, and a bum is a stiff who has been forced out of the working world.[56]

The fighting world has been grist for a series of classic symbolic match-ups whose metaphoric significance would live beyond the bout and even beyond the men themselves. The early part of this century is an era highlighted by the advent of managerial redesign of the industrial workplace, and the replacement of the myth of rugged, socially atomized individualism, with a new liberal corporate vision. The Jack Dempsey-Gene Tunney fights revised and updated the traditional notion of control.

Eliot Gorn wrote of the significance of these bouts, arguing they embodied the norms undergirding a corporate-liberal society. Tunney, the Fighting Marine, stepped forward to confront the Manassa Mauler. Tunney represents the American proletariat who is tamed to bring old "non-rational" labor patterns under control, to obliterate the difference between civic and corporate/ military interest.

Yet there remained a liberating quality to the Manassa Mauler's violence, and, as Dempsey himself acknowledged, the fans had a love-hate relationship with him. Dempsey would vent his wrath

against the growing constraints of a complex society. His embat-
tled will remained opposed to Tunney's disciplined, rational pursuit of goals, and subordination of passions to self-control. Tunney
represented the fulfillment of industrial culture, Dempsey, the
secret impulse to smash through the restrictions imposed by a
bureaucratic society.[57] It is indeed ironic that in the Dempsey-
Tunney "Long Count" fight, the "fight of the century," at least the
century before the Ali-Frazier "Thrilla in Manilla," Tunney, the
disciplined manager's archetype, stole four seconds from a
relentless clock, the same twentieth-century clock that domes-
ticates alienated "stiffs" in the industrial workplace.

David Bathrick points toward the mythology of what is perhaps
most truly the "fight of the century," Joe Louis's defeat of Max
Schmeling. There is an irony embodied in the man who would later
preserve German ideological superiority from the barbarism of Joe
Louis, who was seen in the 1920s as an archetype of democratic
individualism. One Schmeling victory against an Italian fighter in
1928 was described as a "triumph of the democratic principle over
fascist Italy."[58]

In these examples, fighters come to represent monumental struggles
of individuals against forces beyond their control. In both lie the
metaphor of working-class men redefined as participants in struggles larger than themselves, yet involved in self-destructive and
fellow-destructive activities. Struggle for victory becomes a self-
limiting activity, a sort of destructive dance whose aesthetic is the
deification of working-class victory dependent on working-class
defeat. Jack Dempsey said, "when you're fighting, you are fighting
for one thing—money."[59] Dempsey did not project beyond this
self-limiting violence to include the fate of the opponent. As a boy
he had bummed from mining camp to mining camp in the West.
Like many displaced agricultural workers, Dempsey was a part of
the huge lumpen army of disorganized labor. The infant populism
of the Wobblies and their efforts to express solidarity is hardly
present in the alienated instinct-driven self-absorption of the Manassa
Mauler.[60]

As the white, European ethnic working-class boxer is absorbed and replaced by the black and Latino fighters struggling in the late twentieth century, some things change but the dynamics of alienation remain constant. The struggles of those who are successful take place against a backdrop of stunted life chances for the huge majority. We see, in the economically and socially ravaged black belt of the 1930s, Joe Louis emerging, as he did for those blacks who migrated north, as a symbol of hope. Yet the extent of dreams deferred in a violently prejudicial and unjust social order cohabits insidiously with the symbol of power and hope Louis represented. Martin Luther King, Jr. used to tell how, "some time ago one of the southern states adopted a new method of capital punishment. Poison gas supplanted the gallows. In its earliest stages, a microphone was placed inside the sealed death chamber so that scientific observers might hear the words of the dying prisoner, . . . the first victim was a young Negro. As the pellet dropped into the container, and gas curled upward, through the microphone came these words: 'Save me, Joe Louis, save me, Joe Louis. Save me, Joe Louis.' "[61]

The rapaciousness of official reformers is as omnipresent as illegal racket structures. No American institutions have been under greater attack so consistently and passionately as boxing and schooling.[62] Those who suffer from both institutions are not their racketeers, their promoters, or their stars; for the most part they constitute the disenfranchised of our affluent society. They are the children of impoverished ghetto neighborhoods in which anger if not fury, while "dysfunctional," are appropriate.[63] Joyce Carol Oates writes eloquently about the "strategies of self-deception present in Leonard Gardner's novel on boxing, *Fat City*, in which boxing functions as the natural activity of men totally unequipped to comprehend life."[64] She cites other works that operate in the same way: *The Champ*, with the tortured and dim Wallace Beery; *Somebody Up There Likes Me*, the story of Rocky Graziano's "escape" from the streets; *The Harder They Fall*, chronicling the exploitation of a giant South American "stiff" for the enrichment of promoters; Serling's *Requiem for a Heavyweight*, and the heroism and tragedy of Jack Johnson in *The Great White Hope*[65] are all stories of victorious but unheroic men who cannot understand the nature of the struggles they face.

"SIR, THEY PAY ME TO GET THEM IN TROUBLE"

Boxing reform took its latest shape partly as a response to, and certainly in the context of, the death of Korean Deuk Koo Kim in the ring with Ray "Boom Boom" Mancini on November 13, 1982. This is the ring death referred to most often in hearings of that period. This fight also signals itself as a product of its era and intersects strangely with the education reform issues of the time. Ralph Wiley chronicled the pain, dismay, and incomprehension of Mancini upon hearing of Kim's death. He became obsessed with whether people realized that he did not intentionally hurt him.[66] Mancini himself had broken a hand and every thrown punch was itself excruciating. Both Mancini and his handlers reflect the incomprehension as well as the tendency to stereotype the reserve and determination of the Asian fighter: "We figured he'd come out kamikazi."[67] They said "he just wouldn't go down . . . he had great pride."[68] And they describe Mancini's adjustment to an inexperienced fighter, an unknown who had been a bootblack, a tour guide, and baker's assistant before starting a boxing career in 1976. His only hobby was "music listening." He had received just $20,000 to fight Mancini for a shot at the title. Yet, when the investigation began and the light of reform scrutiny began to fall on Mancini and the young Korean who had scrawled on a lampshade in his apartment before the fight, "KILL OR BE KILLED," even as Mancini was left emotionally devastated by Kim's death, his entourage expressed discouragement with the effect of bureaucratic hearings on the tragedy.[69] "They didn't know what a blue-ribbon panel could do now . . . it was not a case of defective equipment or a fighter being allowed to go too far, or any impropriety."[70] It is the sense of incomprehension of realism by participants in a violent struggle, where fairness is a sheen over an invidious and permanently destructive activity.

We were a "nation at risk" from foreign labor and competition; the Asian Pacific Rim was looming to absorb our productive power. A lonely Korean fighter came west, vying for glory against a scion of the last generation of immigrant struggle. Kim and Mancini are archetypes of two new generations of insecurity. Their solidarity was abstracted, absorbed in the deathly effort to destroy each other. When asked whether he knew he had Irish Jimmy Doyle in serious trouble before Doyle's death, Sugar Ray Robinson "looked straight ahead and said, 'sir, they pay me to get them in serious trouble.' "[71]

Bert Sugar was to testify on his feeling that the fight was a serious political mismatch. Disregarding the fact that the fight was a mismatch, he argues that its fatal conclusion could have been prevented by "central control. Were these state commissioners manufacturers of widgets, or distributors of toilet seats, they would have an association . . . a central registry is needed. Maybe an extension of *The Ring* record book . . . " (which Sugar edits).[72] Again, central control will address the appearance of violence by either preventing more of the sloppy advertisements that are the ring deaths, or allow for them to be called the result of fair competition. No mention is made again of the underlying destruction of minds in process.

TOMATO CANS

Michael Shapiro brings us back to the stacks of "opponents," polite semi-intentional losers, upon whose defeat the records of the "horses" are built. He discusses these "tomato cans" in his story of Obie Garnett, a fighter who comes on a bus to Chicago, from Cincinnati where he works in a mill. "He is knocked out and sits in the dressing room while another 'opponent,' Sylvester Wilder, who according to *The Ring* record book once lost thirty-six fights in a row, took a hook to the belly and was counted out. The man who was his second asked Garnett why he was taking these chances for only $175. Garnett, who was in a hurry to catch the bus so he would not miss his shift the next morning replied, 'Christmastime, man.' "[73]

Ronald Levao writes how the risk of death is in some sense an evasion from the "basic degradation" boxers suffer in their performances. Arguably the most successful boxer in history is solemn testimony of how even victory is a degradation. We watch a slow and slurring Muhammad Ali now with sad reflection on the pride and power he once symbolized.[74] Levao notes those "strident voices which urge equality for all, promote and support equal rights, yet watch mute while the literal sacrifice of minority youth unfolds for the profit and delectation of self-styled sportsmen."[75]

KO IN TWELVE

Do we watch with the delectation of self-styled sportsmen while the degradation of minority and working-class youth unfolds in schooling for our profit and pleasure? Is the success of students who contribute to the postindustrial workforce taking place without reference to or interest in the working class whose degradations are the fodder for the success of a few survivors in the intensified competition for high quality work? Christine Shea shows how the success of students in the developing primary labor force may be due to the new intensification of standards and rigor in a "new basics" curriculum. However this alteration, this intensification is "designed only for those increasingly few individuals headed for the primary labor force. For the majority of youngsters headed for the low-paying, dead-end jobs of the secondary labor force, the liberal school reformers promise only to provide a . . . minimal competency, learning how to learn skills."[76] It is a competition where victors are created dependent on the losing fights of underprepared "tomato cans." The "opponents" world is training for the postindustrial world's version of a club fight, a repetitive, deadening, losing proposition for some, a tune-up for the fight that never materializes, as Brando would put in Schulberg's *On the Waterfront* soliloquy, the one "out doors in a ballpark."

Shea documents the distance between the rhetoric of excellence and the reality of education. She cites the "Education commission of the states' report entitled 'action for excellence.' " In it there is a discussion of the new job category of "learning to learn" jobs. The report launches into a detailed description of the newly developed four-tiered occupational classification system that should henceforth be used to classify American workers: (1) unskilled jobs, which can be performed by people with less than today's basic skills, (2) basic jobs, which require today's basics, for example as a clerk in a small noncomputerized store, (3) "Learning to learn" jobs which demand that the worker possess not only basic skills but be capable of acquiring new ones, and (4) professional jobs which require adaptability "learning to learn" (L to L) skills and more sophisticated intellectual skills as well. Most factory and service industry jobs in America today fall into the third category. The skills required for those in the L to L category are "the ability to compute with whole numbers and the ability to use arithmetic computations in solving practical problems." Little intellect is needed for that humble task. Competency in reading demands not only deciphering, but the ability to make inferences. Writing requires not just the ability to write a sentence or paragraph, but to "gather and organize information coherently." Coherent organization is the high water mark of literacy then. Shea rightly shows that highly skilled labor will not likely be in great demand in America's high-tech future, but it "sugar coats" this bitter reality in the soothing rhetoric of "advancing technology, upward mobility, and increasing opportunity."[77]

Thus the latest wave of reform becomes, as in boxing, a simulation of change in service of a much lower goal than what is advertised. Equality and excellence cloak the reality of competition for nonexistent prizes. The chance for victory is skewed by unequal treatment of different competitors to conform to the role they play in the rationalization of economic or institutional stability. Institutions that "serve" participants, the reform councils as well as the governing bodies—like the World Boxing Association (WBA) and the World Boxing Council (WBC)—and the public that enjoys the spectacle, are each in a different way exploiting the participants through the illusion of their protection, thus the comparison to racketeering.

The rhetoric of equal opportunity that characterizes the high-tech reform efforts for a new "excellence" works to uproot the dismal literacy statistics. Yet, as in boxing, the possibilities for educational excellence remain structurally limited to the chosen few. The educational edifice is built on a structure of necessary failure, where job skills and the education required to perform them fall far short of the intellectual potential and the dreams of participants. That this should remain beyond their comprehension is as necessary in education as it is in the ring.

NOTES

1. Joyce Carol Oates, *On Boxing* (New York: Doubleday, 1987), p. 77.

2. Frederic Jameson, "On Cultural Studies," *Social Text* 34 (Spring 1993): 44.

3. Subcommittee on Labor Standards; Committee on Education and Labor, *The Federal Boxing Protection Act of 1983: Hearing on H.R. 1751*, 98th Cong., 1st sess., May 5, 1983, p. 58.

4. Ibid., p. 65.

5. Ibid., p. 100.

6. Ibid., p. 83.

7. Ibid., p. 85.

8. "The Schools after 20 Years," *Education Digest* (January 1989). Thanks to James Anderson for this observation.

9. Saul Cooperman and Leo Klagholtz, "New Jersey's Alternate Route to Certification," *Phi Delta Kappan* (June 1985): 691–95.

10. Ibid., p. 694.

11. Ibid.

12. Lawrence Bershad and Richard J. Ensor, "Boxing in the U.S., Reform, Abolition or Federal Control?: A New Jersey Case Study." *Seton Hall Law Review* 19, no. 865, p. 886.

13. Ibid., p. 868.

14. Ibid., p. 869.

15. Ibid., p. 871.

16. Ibid., p. 866.

17. Ibid., p. 914.

18. Ibid.

19. Ibid., p. 214.
20. Steven R. Heyman, "Ethical Issues in Performance Enhancement Approaches with Amateur Boxers," *The Sport Psychologist* 4 (1990): 50.
21. Ibid.
22. Michele Fine, "A Diary on Privatization and on Public Possibilities," *Educational Theory* 43, no. 1 (Winter 1993): 33.
23. Douglas A. Kellner, *Jean Baudrillard* (Stanford, Calif.: Stanford University Press, 1989), p. 31.
24. Ibid., p. 49. See also Jean Baudrillard, *Mirror of Production* (St. Louis: Telos, 1975).
25. Ibid., p. 56.
26. Ibid., p. 54.
27. Ibid., p. 58.
28. Svi Shapiro, *Between Capitalism and Democracy* (New York: Bergin & Garvey, 1990), p. 130.
29. Ibid.
30. Ernest Kahane and Andrew D. Oram, "Where Computers Are Taking Us in the Education Field," in Christine Shea, Ernest Kahane, and Peter Sola, eds., *The New Servants of Power* (New York: Praeger, 1989), p. 69.
31. Ibid., p. 72.
32. Ibid., p. 73.
33. Peter Sola, "The Corporate Community on the Ideal Business-School Alliance," in Shea, et al., eds., *New Servants*, 1989, p. 75.
34. Richard J. Altenbaugh, "Teachers, Their World, and Their Work: A Review of the Idea of Professional Excellence in School Reform Reports," in Shea, et al., eds., *New Servants*, 1989, p. 168.
35. Ibid., p. 171.
36. José Torres, "Conquer the Violence Within," *Washington Post* "Parade" (May 23, 1993): 5.
37. Charles Leerhsen, "The Man from Culiacan," *New York Times Magazine* (August 29, 1993): 54.
38. Peter M. R. Stirk, *Max Horkheimer: A New Interpretation* (Lanham, Maryland: Barnes and Noble, 1992), p. 140.
39. Ibid., p. 141.
40. Bershad and Ensor, *Boxing in the United States*, p. 874.
41. Ibid., p. 912.
42. Stirk, *Max Horkheimer*, p. 143.
43. Ibid., p. 145.
44. Ibid.
45. Ibid., p. 146.
46. Ibid.
47. Ibid., p. 135.

48. Dale Snauwaert, "Reclaiming the Lost Treasure: Deliberation and Strong Democratic Education," *Educational Theory* 42, no. 3 (Summer 1992): 364.

49. Ibid., p. 364.

50. Subcommittee on Commerce, Transportation and Tourism; Committee on Energy and Commerce, *Bill to Promote Health and Safety in Professional Boxing: Hearings on H.R. 1705*, 99th Cong., 1st sess., July 30, 1985, p. 314.

51. Ibid., p. 316.

52. Ibid., p. 249.

53. Ibid., p. 326.

54. Ibid., p. 327.

55. Gerald Early, "Three Notes Toward a Cultural Definition of Prizefighting," in Joyce Carol Oates and Daniel Halpern, eds., *Reading the Fights* (New York: Henry Holt and Co., 1988), p. 31.

56. Ibid., p. 33.

57. Elliot J. Gorn, "The Manassa Mauler and the Fighting Marine: An Interpretation of the Dempsey-Tunney Fights," in Oates and Halpern, eds., *Reading the Fights*, p. 81.

58. David Bathrick, "Max Schmeling on the Canvas: Boxing as an Icon of Weimar Culture," *New German Critique* (Fall 1990): 113.

59. Oates, *On Boxing*, p. 36.

60. Ibid., p. 87.

61. Ibid., p. 62.

62. Ibid., p. 94.

63. Ibid., p. 63.

64. Ibid., p. 55.

65. Ibid.

66. Ralph Wiley, *Serenity: A Boxing Memoir* (New York: Henry Holt and Co., 1989), p. 120.

67. Ibid., p. 119.

68. Ibid.

69. Bill Barich, "Never Say Never," in Oates and Halpern, eds., *Reading the Fights*, p. 225.

70. Ibid.

71. Wiley, *Serenity*, p. 121.

72. Subcommittee on Commerce, Transportation and Tourism; Committee on Energy and Commerce, *Bill to Establish a Congressional Commission on Boxing: H.R. 1778*, 98th Cong., 1st sess., February 15, 1983, March 18, 1983, p. 214.

73. Michael Shapiro, "Opponents," in Oates and Halpern, eds., *Reading the Fights*, p. 243.

74. Oates and Halpern, *Reading the Fights*, p. 6.

75. Ibid., p. 7.

76. Christine Shea, "Pentagon vs. Multinational Capitalism: The Political Economy of the 1980's School Reform Movement," in Shea et al., eds., *New Servants*, p. 32.

77. Ibid., p. 33.

4

Work Is for Saps:
A New Hawthorne Effect
and the Value of the
Rising Tide of Mediocrity

This chapter is about a couple of fires and an explosion. It is about how the "rising tide of mediocrity" carried the ships of privilege to higher ground. If the high-tech obfuscation of the *Challenger* space story is merged with the earthly violence of boxing reform, this final section speaks to a sort-of conflagration of images, a dialectic synthesis of air and earth to make fire. This fusion of images is dulled by the reality of the human suffering it represents. The two fires and the explosion all happened within a year of each other, half-way around the globe from one another, a fire in Thailand, one in North Carolina, and a demolition in Cicero, Illinois, an old suburb of Chicago. Miles and ages apart in some ways, they are linked by an emerging world labor order, where the fate of working people in both places is made.

In May of 1993, the worst factory fire in history roared through a doll factory in Thailand, killing 240 workers, mostly women. Its earlier rival for industrial infamy was the Triangle Shirtwaist Company fire in New York City in 1911. Triangle captured international attention as an example of the oppressiveness of work conditions for piecework laborers in the garment factory, a staple of the international division of labor that was by 1911 fully developed. The Thailand doll factory fire captured the attention of a column in the inner pages of the *New York Times* for one day, and then vanished.[1]

The similarities between Triangle and the Thailand fire are ironic and important. In both, the labor of women who were underpaid and undervalued for their "flexibility" is being used. In both cases shop doors were locked by managers concerned about pilfering.

The important difference is in the public reaction. Global capitalism has clearly triumphed in its ability to subsume industrial tragedy without much reaction by press or public.

The Thai tragedy is in some ways not the legitimate offspring of that earlier epic fire, however. The global reach of capital is the economic environment to which all reform opinion, in whatever sector of the state, must respond. Education reform dialogue has been developed within the logic of human capital utilization and training. The realities of the global division of labor have been largely obscured behind the radiant glow of high-tech work-force preparation. The fire in Thailand is a smoldering reminder that we must keep squarely in view the actual, not the fictional, nature of working-class chances in the global postindustrial order.

PUTTING PEOPLE FIRST

The central argument of most education reform discourse during this period of global capital flow and general recession has been that of human capital development—education for the "realities" of a global economic competition. If this is true, we must describe exactly whom it is our public-school students are competing with, and what it is they are competing for. How, for example, can working-class children compete for positions in a global market for assembly work without experiencing drastic reductions in security and standard of living? They would be required to be less expensive, yet as "skilled," as the same labor force represented by those who died in the Thai fire, whose wages were roughly $70 per month and who were a threat to subsidize that wage, by pilfering the toy Santas and other dolls for sale in the street.

About a year before the Thai doll factory conflagration, fire broke out at the Imperial Food Products chicken processing plant in Hamlet, a small town in south central North Carolina. As the flames engulfed the plant, workers rushed to the exits only to find six of the nine doors locked, padlocked by the owner to keep them from pilfering chickens. Twenty-five people died and fifty were injured. While this was the worst industrial fire in the state's history, its causes were anything but accidental, and it is not atypical of general conditions in the industrialized southern food processing industry. The poultry industry, which alone employs 20,000 persons, has long been known as a place where workers enjoy few union contracts, and they can, according to state law, be fired for any reason. The $5.30 hourly wage at Imperial Foods was considered good pay for rural North Carolina.[2]

Since the fire in Hamlet, the state has responded with more vigilance in the inspection of sites, and there is a noticeable new momentum for the organization of poultry workers, a formidable challenge in a state where 30 percent of the full-time work force earns less than $12,000 per year—poverty wages for a family of four.[3] This export of assembly production and industrial agriculture to rural areas and low labor cost areas should have a measurable effect on how critical educators assess the relationship between schooling reform proposed and actual economic opportunity for students.

The continued rationalization of labor, the export of production, and adjustment of labor market size and quality through immigration continue to be the real "heartbeat of America." Its results are continuing on a path that for the American working class was only broken by the artificial production and market monopolies associated with world wars. This "deindustrialization" process is perfectly compatible with the logic of corporate capital accumulation, yet it produces working-class suffering, expanding underemployment, and increasing proletarianization of managerial personnel. The flow of capital to these ends is causing widespread economic stagnation and working-class immiserization, yet it continues to be the miseducation of public-school children which is blamed for these disturbing changes.[4]

We have in the cases of Thailand and North Carolina seen capital flow toward poverty and seen it do little to ameliorate the objective conditions of the working class. Arguments for a "world class" science and math education, the increase in state assessment, an extended school day or any other frequently cited reform idea would have little positive effect on the ability of a venture capitalist in the southern labor market to find suitable human capital for work required in this sector of the division of labor.

Despite the rhetorical cries for higher skills in the work force, the de-skilling of industrial labor has proceeded along with the global expansion of capitalism. These are the "precondition of the globalization of the labor process. In this manner, the process of de-skilling in the advanced capitalist countries, having taken several decades to develop, finds its way into the readily transformed structure of many third world economies . . . universal de-skilling, aside from its hegemonic appeal, allows for co-existence of the highest level of technology and the lowest possible labor cost . . . as a result, the rising complexity of technology in the production process does not pose a physical limit to raising the exploitation and the working classes globally."[5]

Production processes in assembly work are increasingly rationalized globally in response to advanced computer, telecommunications, and automation techniques, and by expanding the pool of unemployed and increasing the premium placed on managerial control of production processes at ever higher levels of concentration. In the "Adam Smith Address on Education—Labor Force Quality and the Economy," University of Chicago economist Gary Becker presents for us an important mainstream picture of the actual relationship between education and human capital requirements of industry. Becker's talk illustrates a number of key issues and contradictions. Nearly everything, for Becker, is capital: "schooling, a computer training course, expenditures on medical care, lectures on the virtues of punctuality and honesty are capital too in the sense that they improve health, raise earnings, or even add to a person's appreciation of literature over much of his or her lifetime."[6] For Becker, expenditures on education are capital investments. Return on investment is expected, however, to come primarily in the form of profit and corporate value. If the worker experiences a benefit, either personally or financially, it is a side effect, neither undesirable nor required.

Becker raises an important issue when he takes theoretical exception to Marxist influenced notions of capital exploitation. "If capital exploits labor, does human capital exploit labor too?" he asks. "Are skilled workers and unskilled workers pitted against each other in the alleged class conflict between labor and capital?"[7] He argues that key investments in human capital were instrumental in the continuing growth of per capita incomes during the past hundred years in the United States, parts of Europe, and Japan. However a significant part of this analysis rests on the precise effects of productivity increases on working people, not on a generalized "per capita" assessment where increases in incomes are coexistent with the industrialization of agriculture, and the extension of capitalist wage labor through industrialization and rationalization of labor.

Becker argues that "it is clear that all countries that manage persistent growth in incomes also have large increases in the education and training of their labor force."[8] He neglects to mention the degree to which the rationalization and industrial control of production in modern economies also requires the development of a credentials market for the adjustment and control of the size of the labor cohorts "coming on line." That this credential market is concomitant to increased school attendance should be no surprise, for this is the embedded "rationalization" for the value of credentials. However, the expansion of scientific and technical knowledge associated with rationalized labor and automated production works against the requirement that an expanded working cohort with high-level reasoning and scientific and/or technical literacy is required for profit. Rather, this training value is ever more concentrated, or as Becker notes, "embodied in people—scientists, scholars, technicians, business economists, managers and other contributors to output."[9] If increases in productivity are beneficial, the benefits accrue to the specialized class, whose labor is devoted in part to production techniques that can operate independently or less dependently on expensive labor.

Becker notes the correlation between "persistent growth in incomes and training of their labor force. First elementary-school education becomes universal, then high-school education spreads rapidly, and finally children from middle income and poorer families begin going to college."[10] He fails to mention how higher education is complicit with capitalist enterprise in the manufacture of the credentials gauntlet where credential acquisition is a form of valuable merchandise to be traded for the right to fill out a job application, more than the sign that the education for which it stands has been even an imprecise training for the actual job one will be performing.

Near the end of his address Becker deals with the natural outgrowth of this set of issues, and does so without seeming to be aware of it. Human capital is not a problem when dealing with the primary productive work force. This is the work force that has not been displaced or immiserated by the flow of capital to low labor cost sites, or the automation of working- and middle-class jobs. "What then is the United States human capital problem?" Becker asks. His answer? "It is the lower 30 percent or so of high-school students, who either do not finish school or who are in the bottom quartile of high-school graduates."[11] He talks first about how the real wage rates for that sector have fallen 30 percent since 1970, and uses that as an indicator of the plight of these students. However, while addressing an audience of business economists, he quickly moves from the plight of the lower 30 percent to the plight of business. The problem for capital is that, lacking credentials, this cohort cannot put labor supply pressure on the cohort above, working thereby to keep wages down. Their uselessness in this capacity, for Becker, can be solved by their replacement by higher skilled (read credentialed) immigrants, who should be allowed into the country under more liberalized immigration legislation. He says that he would like to describe what can be done to help workers at the lower end of the skill distribution end compete more effectively.[12] Yet he proceeds to disclose a plan that will only equip them to compete *less* effectively in their own interest, but more effectively in the interest of business that will benefit by the "increase (in) the quality at the lower end of the labor force without requiring much additional public spending. The easiest action conceptually, though not politically, would be to reorient (indeed) immigration policy to admit many more younger skilled workers."[13]

Becker's talk would please Adam Smith, if it were as unambiguous as Smith had been on the capacity of the division of labor under capitalism to produce workers, paraphrasing from *The Wealth of Nations* as stupid as it is possible for a human being to become. Where Becker rhetorically asks early in the address whether it is possible for human capital to exploit workers, the answer is yes, as long as the body and energy of this "human" is objectified in the service of capital by virtue of its exploitability, worker against worker. In Becker's talk we see the continued theme of reform where the blame for working-class misery is reassigned, away from the structure of capital formation during this postindustrial global crisis, back to the workers themselves, whose displacement and misery is blamed on their lack of literacy, a type of high-status academic literacy, for which there is no direct use in most current forms of labor.

THE HAWTHORNE EFFECT

I would like to shift to an explosion, or rather an implosion, which occurred in Cicero, Illinois, in April of 1994. The fires mentioned previously were symptomatic of labor conditions where assembly, or in the chicken case, disassembly workers are exploited. The demolition, planned and methodical, of the Western Electric Hawthorne telephone works is an outgrowth of the global flow of electronics assembly and the automation concurrent with the high-tech movement. That it happened at Hawthorne is particularly intriguing and germane to this story. Hawthorne embodies so much that is at the heart of the issues central to reform of education and its alliance with industry in this century. During the 1920s and 1930s Western Electric's Hawthorne works employed 40,000 people in a town whose population was not much bigger. It was the largest telephone factory in the world. During prohibition, Al Capone's headquarters were just a half-block away, and Hawthorne's success was no small source of pride in a town known the world over as a gangster town. While it closed finally in 1986 and was demolished in 1994, Hawthorne represents several crystalline ironies.[14] First, Western Electric's fame comes not mainly for its contribution to the advancement of postindustrial technologies, but to industrial human relations research, which was pioneered there. The Hawthorne studies of management-worker interaction contributed to the founding of industrial psychology as a discipline and to the neoliberal effort to develop techniques that would ameliorate the management-labor frictions which threatened capital throughout the late nineteenth and early part of the twentieth centuries. Its demise tells "of the landscape's change from smokestacks to shopping malls, of electronics once made in a blue-collar Chicago suburb and now made overseas. And of young people shifting their attention from factory bells to Taco Bells."[15]

The research at Hawthorne was pioneered by Elton Mayo of Harvard University. In the most famous of the studies, the one on lighting effects, a serendipitous discovery led to an adjustment in experimental focus. In this study, researchers sought to discover the effect of lighting on worker output. They found that if supervisors increased lighting in the plant, the workers would work harder, but complain; when lights were dimmed in response to complaints, output rose even more. The conclusion was that it was not the lighting they should focus on but on the fact that workers liked the *feeling* that management was listening to them. Establishing this feeling was found to be the best predictor of ongoing productive work. Finding ways to give workers the illusion that their opinion matters to management became the keystone for the science of industrial psychology, and affected the development of group dynamics as a social science focus.[16]

It is precisely this sort of worker involvement in the discourse of production that is the heart of current arguments in education reform linked to the need for total quality management, quality circles and cooperative reorganization of high-tech work, and midmanagement of all sorts. Along with privatization, raised standards, and state testing, all of these moves are in the vanguard of today's discussion in school reform. How ironic it is that this effort was no barrier to the demise of the electronics enterprise that pioneered it. Even now the wholesale attempt to resurrect this kind of enterprise is proceeding on the Pacific Rim, leaving workers in Cicero to fight for minimum wage and part-time work in the shopping mall which will replace the factory, and be named after it.

The classic study that recapitulates the Hawthorne studies was *Management and the Worker*. For years after its publication there developed an academic cottage industry devoted to its findings. For example, in *Hawthorne Revisited*, a critical review of this literature and a retrospective on *Management and the Worker*, Landsberger argues that the Hawthorne experiments are directly responsible for pioneering the small-group dynamics movement of which quality circles and work redesign efforts today are an offshoot. Cooperative education and the synthetic and interpretive literacy of the reform rhetoric is supposed to be a key brick in the rebuilding of our productive capacity. We are supposed to produce students for this "new world of work." The rhetoric of education reform support and industrial technique must be questioned when the technique fails to work in the place it was invented. The issue at Hawthorne is not plant obsolescence either. As Becker mentioned, as if oblivious to its consequences, it is the management-constructed exploitation of worker by worker.[17]

It was Elton Mayo's belief that "the submergence of the self is necessary if the worker is to achieve psychological satisfaction in a modern factory."[18] Landsberger cites Freeman, a Mayo critic, who argued that civilized man has developed capacities away from the ability to submerge himself.[19] "When we set industrial co-operation against a larger psychological background than that of profit and earning a living alone we cannot escape the fact that it offends as well as serves civilized man."[20] The goal of human relations in this context is countereducation if, by education we understand the importance of knowledge. The purpose here is psychological manipulation of worker awareness and understanding in the interest of the organization. Underlying this is either deep suspicion of the capacity for reasoned consciousness or a deep understanding that his or her reason must be obscured due to its power to emerge on its own, as separate from corporate interest.

There have been numerous recent efforts at re-skilling work, and the movement toward work resocialization and organizational redesign. This redesign has been instigated through efforts to increase productivity, yet "even in countries like Sweden, where organized labor is strong, employee participation in decision making at the factory level has remained quite limited."[21] Contemporary working conditions are characterized by extremes in capital flow, reorganization, and automation of work. In the former instance, the flow of capital is away from wherever workers have established decent conditions, yet conditions that are more expensive to employers. In the latter case, redesigns of work have not often called upon the requirement that workers mobilize the significantly greater measure of those capacities nurtured by the kind of education advised by the excellence movement. Peter Alic argues the earlier generation of workplace machines were in fact less transparent and more amenable to comprehension than computer-mediated machines, which when they do not engage human rationality, simply transcend it.[22]

The Hawthorne studies emerged in an era in which capital was busy employing and supporting the efforts of social scientists to help solve the labor crises that threatened industrial peace. To some degree, capital dodged the bullet of further labor unrest due in part to more sophisticated management techniques and educational interventions. War mobilization looms larger for its effect in the

United States to partly unify the interest of big labor and capital, both interested in the domination of international commodity production. However, the current decline of U.S. global industrial hegemony during the present stage of global capitalist relations has led to "a growing divergence between the material interests of labor and capital. The once shared interest . . . is now seen as a source of job loss, demands for concessions and union busting. The economic conditions for post World War II accommodation of capital (by labor) are over."[23]

The Hawthorne experiments were bellwether studies used in support of the progressive education movement, and a predecessor to the whole raft of worker "empowerment" arguments central to sophisticated management strategies. It is interesting to see this icon of education research and industrial progress reduced to bricks, dust, and twisted girders as part of global capital mobility in search of increased productivity. For in point of fact, education has little to do with falling living standards, certainly less than the flight of capital to places where it seeks not the savvy of well-educated workers, but conditions of industrial servitude.

Paul Sweezy points to the fact that since the 1970s there has been an enormous surplus of industrial capacity with plants running at only 79 percent. "Despite the boom of the 1980s, he reminds us, real wages did not go up . . . incomes of working people at the lower levels have been steady or declining and at the lowest levels, they've dropped a lot. At the top five or ten percent they've increased amazingly. Income distribution is worse than it has ever been in American history."[24] He points to that part of the crisis that manifests itself in stagnation, through overcapacity and overproduction.

In earlier periods overproduction and surpluses were handled through the medium of labor enhancing technology. This form of machine rationalization required workers in this country to run the machines. Despite falling wages "they were still able to afford the necessities of life and thus maintain the market. The labor enhancing technology of the past period, however, is more and more being replaced by the labor eliminating technology of the present period.

. . . The fluctuations in poverty and cyclical unemployment of the earlier period are increasingly giving way to the polarization of wealth and poverty and growing permanent unemployment of the present period."[25]

When the National Task Force on Education for Economic Growth argued that "school and business leaders should develop partnerships to advance school improvement," their call came as a response to the increasing need to "harmonize" school efforts with work requirements.[26] Svi Shapiro concentrates on the perceived productivity crisis that drove and still drives much current educational reform. He reminds us of the *Report of the Task Force on Federal Elementary and Secondary Education Policy* sponsored by the Twentieth Century Fund, which said the "public school should ensure the availability of large numbers of skilled and capable individuals without which we cannot sustain a complex and competitive economy."[27] And, according to the National Commission on Excellence in Education (NCEE) report, "the citizen is dismayed at a steady fifteen-year decline in industrial productivity, as one great American industry after another falls to world competition."[28] He notes how, as a response to this concern, science and technology education rose to the top of the list of cures. There is, however, too little discussion of the real reasons for productivity decline and competitiveness, beyond the bromides offered by blue ribbon reports. The reality is much more complicated and requires something more than a "re-tooling" of the worker through education.

New Jersey is another example of a crippled industrial behemoth whose morale and economy were being patched up with a mix of erstwhile rackets in high-tech glitz and gambling casinos. Both are glamorous ways to bolster sagging economies and avoid tax increases. New Jersey rises to the top once again. A number of Japanese and Korean electronics firms have located along the higher-education corridor on New Jersey's U.S. Route One. State- and foundation-subsidized research from Princeton, Rutgers, and others are cited as the prime reason for the location of these firms.[29] Likewise the casino industry explodes at the start of Route One, as

the lodestone of job and resource generation for the depleted
Atlantic City. Yet, both of these developments have not altered
Atlantic City's 16.4 percent of New Jersey's 8.4 percent unemployment rate, one of the nation's highest.[30] The two fires and
implosion of Hawthorne help to illuminate conditions of labor in
a sector seemingly far removed from the "cutting edge" industries
of Route One in New Jersey. However, it is precisely related to the
way in which capital roams the earth, searching for opportunities
to exploit both cheap labor and labor-replacing machinery.

A GOOD ATTITUDE

The successes predicted for American participation in the postindustrial revolution are at best ambiguous. Michael Marien
reviews the twentieth-century literature on future visions of industrial and postindustrial society. He characterizes them as best
described by Daniel Bell's postindustrial "service society." Yet,
this vision is then divided between that society as "a technological,
affluent" society and a "decentralized agrarian economy following
in the wake of a failed industrialism."[31] Few freehold farms are
springing from the rubble of factories like Hawthorne, so it is better
to concentrate on the discussion surrounding the prospects for the
centralized technological state. On one hand, much has been
written about the service society's prospects and our educational
preparation for it presupposes expanded opportunity for what
R. H. Tawney called the class of "brain workers" who would
populate a postindustrial economy. For Tawney, writing in 1920,
this class would grow as a proletariat not an elite, resulting "from
the concentration of business, the spread of organisation, and the
application of science to industry."[32]

The proletarianization of this class has consequences for both
their life chances for happiness and their ability to function with
civic, rather than consumer, consciousness. We must come to grips
with the need for a debate on the educational needs of a class of
skilled workers who will not enjoy a particularly rewarding standard of living. Erica Schoenberger writes of the ambiguous future

of professional and technical workers in manufacturing. She discusses the logic of automation and technology in post-Fordist computer and artificial-intelligence-mediated manufacturing. These technologies allow for product differentiation while maintaining economies of scale, and this "capacity for strategic intervention suggests the desirability of retaining some relatively skilled workers on the shop floor. But the numbers required will be small compared with the boom years of Fordism—in short they will not compensate for the rationalization and restructuring that has already taken place.[33] She stresses the availability of low-cost, relatively high-skill labor forces in the periphery—Singapore, South Korea, Taiwan, Hong Kong.[34] The ceaseless ability and desire of the flow of capital, however, has already taken its toll on the workers of one of these "Asian tigers."

Forbes magazine profiles one ambitious entrepreneur, Johnny Lau, Hong Kong electronics firm owner. Founder and chairman of Tomei International, Lau, forty-four, one of the world's largest makers of low- and medium-end audio equipment. Moderate increases in living standards have begun to scare businesses like Lau's away from Hong Kong to China's mainland. "Hong Kong has become too civilized," says Lau. "You have to pay unemployment benefits, make social security and labor insurance payments and give maternity leave. In the People's Republic of China you pay a dollar for a dollar of labor; in Hong Kong you pay $1.50."[35] Tomei now has 90 percent of its production in China, where 20,000 workers, most of them subcontracted, toil in its ten factories. The wages, at $60 to $80 per month are about 10 percent of Hong Kong levels.[36] If an important part of the education process is one of "civilization" then civilization that includes the ability to see what will, paraphrasing Jefferson, secure your freedom and happiness, then it is a bad investment for one high-tech honcho. Replace civilization with domestication, or redefine civilization *as* domestication, and you have an improved goal, one set in the interests not of workers and citizens but owners and stockholders.

A major part of the science of human relations instigated by Mayo at Hawthorn depended on the stimulation of loyalty through the illusion of worker management. This challenge is central in an economy whose remaining production jobs either exist as third-world sweatshops or where workers at the point of production find what remains of their craft eroded further by the mediation of artificial intelligence and computer manufactories.[37] The final labor sector, the vaunted service sector is in fact responsible for the large majority of new jobs. As computers become more "user friendly" and "menu-driven," the demand for complex human interactions erodes.[38] This new de-skilling keeps capital fluid and investors happy as long as overproduction remains below crisis levels.

In fact demand for professional and technical occupations has dropped from 30 percent growth in the decade 1960–1970, to 17.1 percent in the years 1982–1995.[39] High-tech and services will not be an employment panacea, and one can envision with the globalization of capital, the immiseration of the working people coinciding with the continuing prosperity of the stock markets.

The basic issue for educators here, above all others, is how to make sense of an official information mill churning out portentous calls for skills related to work that is becoming scarce, if not extinct, for a large portion of our students. If many of the cautionaries are correct regarding postindustrial conditions, the chief labor problem facing business is how to stimulate consumption among consumers who not only have no money, but have no property worth enough to leverage against credit—that fuel for today's vibrant consumer economy.

The stranger that Maxine Greene was talking about was not in the classroom, having been replaced by teacher as goon—labor domesticator in the world of reproduction. The goon has been re-upholstered as a sort of user-friendly, if schizoid, standardized-test teacher/cooperative facilitator, in the swamps of students' minds so drained by consumerism that false consciousness would not even grow.

Postmodern work is epitomized in the pages of *Bad Attitude*, an anthology collected in the quarterly *Processed World*. Published in San Francisco, this manifesto of anomie is "dedicated to all the subversive spirits languishing in lonely, useless jobs every-where."[40] It makes no effort to be evenhanded but in an off-beat way documents well some of the emerging work conditions that prevail in the United States. Seeking to "illuminate the underside of the information age, it is especially plangent when describing the immiseration, and proletarianization of managerial and "high-skill" high-tech work—the "cutting edge," as it were, of a new economy.

An enormous part of this edge is high-tech interface labor done on a consulting or temporary basis. This is the techno-sweated labor, which is more fashionable and certainly tidier than deboning a chicken or painting a thousand doll eyebrows to make the "bogey."[41] Christopher Winks (pseud.) describes a splinter off the plank of this kind of work in "Manuscript Found in a Typewriter." In it, he accentuates Barbara Garson's claim that the work oppressions of routinization, de-skilling, and loss of control, which have long been the province of the "back office," are threatening the work in the executive front office.[42] Winks describes his work for a franchising operation that contracts out secretarial services to clients. He was set to work transcribing a legal document from dictation. This kind of clerical labor was long the work of skilled front-office secretaries, with reasonably extensive autonomy. Now in an effort to provide an "atmosphere" of production control, Winks describes that ubiquitous material that outlines the illusion of personal, even homey space, and defines the impermanence of postindustrial mobile capital—the office fabric partition. These are the soft walls of the "office of the future"[43] where "human relations" are simply obfuscations of older corrosive hierarchies.

The underbelly of the vaunted explosion in service occupations is occupied by the "temporary" business services industry. It experienced more growth than any other industry during the 1980s. Despite receiving little attention, this "contingent" work force is the main provider of subcontracted labor.[44] Robert Parker argues that this proletarianization of clerical labor, which began with the "back office" and was documented by C. Wright Mills and Harry Braverman, is evolving and entering a heightened phase. The introduction of labor-saving devices, such as standardized, menu-driven word processing has further hampered workers in their ability to exert discretion in their daily work or to manifest crafts not embodied in the standardized "user friendly" equipment.[45]

Also employers have moved aggressively to integrate temporary workers into multiple phases of their operation.[46] The management mediated the exploitation of workers by "human capital" that Becker alluded to earlier is evident. Now, with the expansion of day labor, subcontracting, part-time, and temporary employment workers are further subdivided by their schedules, and the working conditions they must endure, limiting opportunity for worker solidarity and organizational ability. This is the much vaunted "flexibility" demanded by the new labor order alluded to time and time again in the education reform literature. When Bill Clinton on the stump discussed the need for workers to "retrain" several times in a lifetime of shifting careers, this is a big part of what he meant.

In "Kelly Call Girl" Laura Fraser reminds us of the varied uses of high-synthesis, high-literacy— "world class" education as she recounts the minutes after logging in on her personal computer in time for central word processing to check her electric clock punch. As she guzzles coffee, another temporary, Rosa, drops unopened mail on her desk. Two magazines are on the top, *Wall Street Journal* and *TempoRite*, the magazine of the Kelly Girls. Rosa tells her that the boss says if you hit a lull you can read *TempoRite* but not the *Journal*. Fraser clips articles from each—from the *W.S.J.*: "Schultz's Meeting Won't Spark Talks With Nicaragua," "The 1985 Continental-Its Looks Raise Expectations, Its Luxury and Technology Fulfill Them," "Union Carbide is Fined 3.9 Million by U.S. Over Test Report," "An Appraisal: Technology Stocks Advance as Industrials Hit Record," "South Africa Free Funds Entail Risk, Study Says," and from *TempoRite* "Isn't Your Secretary Important To You?" "Every sixty days, 16,000 top executives give their secretaries a new learning system called BIZ." "Your secretaries' productivity is linked to yours." "Secretaries are entitled to and need affirmation of the key role they play . . .

along with ongoing encouragement and systematic assistance in learning how to become more valuable on the job."[47]

It does not take much imagination to understand the value of high literacy regarding Laura's ability to interpret the meaning of the *Wall Street Journal* and the importance of her access to *TempoRite*. The value to her and the value to her employer are two very different things.

WORK IS FOR SAPS

Decentralization then, the creation of the mosaic of contingent work, is tantamount to the institutionalization of piecework as a structure. When Herbert Kohl said, "very few people are needed to do the creative work in these (high-tech related) fields,"[48] he could have been talking about the congeries of reprocessed toil passing for the kind of midmanagement work thought to be the reward for years of school attendance. It is not as much that very few workers are needed, but that very few *persons* are.

There is something Promethean in the search for the engineers' grail—the near total elimination of human labor.[49] The dystopia of 1984 is balanced in the popular mind by the utopia of flexible decentralized and now intelligent computers. Computers are only a part of the issue. Their part in the replacement of labor for toil is emblematic of the current age, but the usual suspects of labor exploitation through de-skilling and capital mobility are still with us. We must, as educators, not forget that education is that collaboration—the construction of persons and creative labor was always rife with ethical and social overtones, and "work was not mere toil or unending drudgery, but salvation."[50] A true work ethic is production that is fit for persons. Sadly, the rhetorical cooperation between the education industry, the state and corporate interests have packaged literacy and numeracy as a sort of theater, reprocessed as a distraction from the theft of rewarding work that is taking place right under the noses of workers in the United States. As real work disappears and standards of living fall for nearly everyone, "mediocrity" and "illiteracy" become the decoy. The education industry created a blaze of gunfire in its direction, as the kind of work for which literacy has any real meaning is exported or imploded in the ceaseless movement of capital to increase "productivity" by increasing workers' exploitation of workers and automated competition for remaining "brain workers."

In that classic gangster film *Little Caesar*, Edward G. Robinson, playing a Capone-ish rackets boss, Johnny Rocco, gets grilled by the coppers for his misspent life, and at one point they ask him why he doesn't get a job, like everybody else. To that he barks, "Work is for saps!"[51] The Johnny Roccos of today, however, are not the ones trading in new drugs, or running after the small change rackets, chasing loans to bad gamblers, as the state of Illinois has commandeered the gaming rackets, casinos, and the lotteries—ironically on a promise to use the rake-off to pay for the education that cannot be paid for by out-of-work taxpayers in Cicero.

History allows us to imagine the real Capone, paring his nails, watching the streams of clock-punchers filing in and out of Hawthorne every day, with dreams of a better life for their grandchildren, and allows us to fast-forward to the day Cicero loses forty thousand jobs in a fifteen-second demolition, jobs exported, jobs eliminated, in the midst of the ballyhooed high-tech revolution. If work means an individual's ability to invest in a stable future for children, then maybe Johnny Rocco was right.

NOTES

1. P.T. Bangsberg, "Asia Pays High Price for Success as Lax Safety Rules Claim Victims," *Journal of Commerce and Commercial* (May 25, 1993): 1–2. China reported 15,000 industrial deaths; Hong Kong and India also report high rates.

2. "The Failure to Inspect," *U.S. News and World Report* (September 16, 1991): 11.

3. A discussion of the unemployment and underemployment that drives oppressive working conditions in Asia appears in ibid. The labor sector, directly below that of the chicken workers in Hamlet, is characterized by conditions of squalor and virtual servitude in the Southern migrant agricultural work force. See Ron Chekusiuk, "Peonage for Peach Pickers," *The Progressive* (December 1992): 22–23.

4. Jerry Lembke, "Class Formation and Class Capacities: A New Approach to the Study of Labor and the Labor Process, " in Berch Berberoglu, *The Labor Process and Control of Labor* (Westport, Conn.: Praeger, 1993), pp. 1–20, p. 15.

5. Cyrus Bina and Chuck Davis, "Transnational Capital, the Global Labor Process and the International Labor Movement," in Berberoglu, *The Labor Process*, pp. 152–170, p. 154.

6. Gary S. Becker, "The Adam Smith Address on Education—Labor Force Quality and the Economy," *Business Economics* 27, no. 1: 7–12.

7. Ibid.

8. Ibid., p. 8.

9. Ibid.

10. Ibid.

11. Ibid., p. 10.

12. Ibid., p. 11.

13. Ibid.

14. Tom Pelton, "Hawthorne Works Glory Now Just So Much Rubble," *Chicago Tribune* (April 18, 1994), sec. 1, p. 1, 6.

15. Ibid.

16. See F. J. Roethlisberger and William J. Dickson, *Management and the Worker* (New York: John Wiley and Sons, Inc., 1964); also Henry A. Landsberger, *Hawthorne Revisited: "Management and the Worker" Its Critics and Developments in Human Relations in Industry* (Ithaca: Cornell University Press, 1958).

17. Landsberger, *Hawthorne Revisited*, pp. 1–7.

18. Ibid., p. 35.

19. Ibid., p. 36.

20. Ibid.

21. John A. Alic, "Who Designs Work?: Organizing Production in an Age of High Technology," *Technology and Society* 12 (1990): 301–317, 303.

22. Ibid.

23. Bina and Davis, "Transnational Capital," p. 159.

24. Barbara Koeppel, Interview with Paul Sweezy, *The Progressive* (May 1992): 234.

25. Walda Katz-Fishman and Jerome Scott, "The Labor Process and Class Struggle: Political Responses to the Control and Exploitation of Labor," in Berberoglu, *The Labor Process*, pp. 171–192.

26. Svi Shapiro, *Between Capitalism and Democracy: Educational Policy and the Crisis of the Welfare State* (New York: Bergin & Garvey, 1990), p. 131.

27. Ibid., p. 134.

28. Ibid.

29. N.R. Kleinfield, "Legal Gambling faces Higher Odds," *New York Times* (August 29, 1993): 3.

30. Ibid.

31. Michael Marien, "The Two Visions of Post-Industrial Society," *Futures* (October 1977): 415–431, 416.

32. Ibid., p. 48.

33. Erica Schoenberger, "The Ambiguous Future of Professional and Technical Workers in Manufacturing: Some Hypotheses," *Acta Sociologica* 31, no. 3 (1988): 241–247, 242.

34. Ibid., p. 243.

35. Andrew Tanzer, "Cantonese Conquistadores," *Forbes Magazine* (March 2, 1992): 56–58, 56.

36. Ibid., p. 58.

37. Dennis C. Scheck, "High Technology: Job Skill Requirements and Job Opportunities," *Humanity and Society* 11, no. 3 (1987): 152–163, 153.

38. Samuel E. Bleecker, "The Information Age Office," *Futurist* (January/February, 1991): 19–20. Bleecker is perhaps here alluding to the traditional female office worker, now "manning" the office of the future, and who is now also surrounded at work by an iconography of "menus," emptying the "trash," cleaning "windows," changing "styles," and so on. Bleecker argues, counter to the high synthetic intelligence arguments of current reform rhetoric, that the postindustrial office will soon be a "landing site surrounded by intelligent information appliances . . . intelligent machines that have all the power of a mini-computer but are as easy to use as a toaster."

39. Scheck, *High Technology*, p. 160.

40. Chris Carlsson, ed., *Bad Attitude: The Processed World Anthology* (London: Verso, 1990).

41. The "bogey" is worker slang for the number of units of labor set as goal to satisfy management for a given period of work. At Hawthorne, 6,600 wiring connections per day, or 914 per hour made the bogey. Exceeding this, "rate busting" set a higher standard of production, good for management, bad for workers, and caused shop-floor friction while workers competed for the favor of bosses. See Landsberger, *Hawthorne Revisited*, pp. 414–417.

42. Barbara Garson, *The Electronic Sweatshop: How Computers Are Transforming the Office of the Future into the Factory of the Past* (New York: Simon and Schuster, 1988), p. 9.

43. Christopher Winks (pseud.), "Manuscript Found in a Typewriter," in Chris Carlsson, ed., *Bad Attitude: Processed World Anthology* (London: Verso, 1990), pp. 19–22, p. 20.

44. Robert E. Parker, "The Labor Force in Transition: Growth of the Contingent Workforce in the United States," in Berberoglu, *The Labor Process*, pp. 116–136, p. 123.

45. Ibid., p. 128.

46. Ibid., p. 132.

47. Laura Fraser, "Kelly Call Girl," *Processed World*, pp. 26–32, p. 27.

48. Louis Michaelson, interview with Herb Kohl, "Computer Education = Processed Kids?" *Processed World*, pp. 211–218, p. 217.

49. Tom Athanasiou, "Mind Games," *Processed World*, pp. 200–210, p. 206.

50. James B. Gilbert, *Work Without Salvation: America's Intellectuals and Industrial Alienation* (Baltimore: Johns Hopkins University Press, 1977).

51. See also "Why Work?" *Utne Reader* (July/August 1988): 47–71.

5

And a Pedagogy
from the Surreal

In education one is dealing with children in whom one has to inculcate certain habits of diligence, precision, poise (even physical poise), ability to concentrate on specific subjects, which cannot be acquired without the mechanical repetition of disciplined and methodical acts.

Antonio Gramsci[1]

Since these mysteries are beyond us, let's pretend we're organizing them.

Jean Cocteau[2]

Many of the conditions imbedded in the case chapters reflect an ongoing story of the power of ideology to teach and direct and to see education as a "mouth moving in the service of capital." They speak to the limitations placed on the capacity of citizens to realize an educational discourse that maximizes human potential in the service of humane purposes. As such these chapters participate in the long discussion of how culture and the educational state glow in reflection of the crasser impulses of production, distribution, and consumerism in the absence of a classic public sphere.

This chapter is an attempt to fashion a discussion regarding pedagogical responses in light of the impediments implied in previous chapters. This chapter raises questions and offers a response. I will argue that most bets are off regarding a sure way to teach for critical educators. But some discussion regarding direction is in order. All the attempts at privatization, the heightened bureaucratization of assessment, and state goal setting collaborate with the mystification of a credentials market that cannibalizes working-class children in the service of a shrinking and frightened middle-class "meritocracy." The best discussions of a direction for critical pedagogy during the 1980s came from those who suggested a "language of possibility," but even they undersold the enormity of the obstacles facing consciousness development and intellectual task setting for critical educators. They took on the frozen legacy of reproduction theory and offered hope. This chapter is a discussion of the place of hope, and a revival of those pedagogical possibilities imbedded in the best elements of reproduction theory.

It is the argument here that any counterhegemonic argument must face a new and confusing power of a bewildering array of spectacular distractions from and justification for unwarranted suffering. The possibilitarian argument was right to criticize cynicism and opportunism of our academic privilege, and to decry the cottage industry of educational radicalism which does not offer a return on theoretical investment. But for serious radical scholars, I believe that it is an adequate return on investment to remain in the problem identification business, to ward off unsubstantiated claims of possible praxis, and to work toward outlining the actual conditions of restriction and obfuscation that stand in the way of social change.

Many of us labor in a minefield of dangerous opportunities as academics teaching teachers. We are too close to an ability to profit from the credentials market which blossoms paradoxically as possibilities for satisfying employment become more scarce, depending more and more on rationalization of schooling to cloak diminishing opportunity. We are threatened with overconfidence that our pronouncements are radicalizing students engaged in that most bourgeois privilege, credentials acquisition and the new job applications you can fill because of *that*, not your newfound ability to articulate a theoretical rationale for social change.

Many of the radical educators involved in the sad family war over the relative darkness of reproduction theory are themselves liberally educated scholars who somehow sneaked into the mostly middlebrow world of normal school education. As such they are liable to forget their brief or nonexistent time in contemporary public elementary or comprehensive high schools, either as student or teacher, and are prone to forget the real way such schools have rewarded the pleasant, efficient "official" teachers who routinely ply their trade in those walls. How many themselves fled those walls (or were themselves cashiered) when hopes for solidarity with politically naive liberals and hostile and socially reactionary conservatives were dashed in one way or another? For how many were radical scholarship and solidarity of some kind or another found only in the oasis of their graduate classes in education foundations, history, sociology, or philosophy and not back in the teacher's lounge? I have spent enough time in both the worlds of practical teaching and education scholarship to know something about it, and seeing how thinly stretched and fiercely competitive is the web of radical education scholarship, I do not bet on it as a big favorite in the race toward human liberation.

Possibilitarian energy must meet some difficult conditions to be meaningfully realized. There are many kinds of hope, and I believe, differing from the possibilitarian argument, that one bad kind of hope is a manic hope in the unjustifiable. While it is more immediately energizing than desperation, warranted desperation can *lead* to a form of hope realistically matched to the level of sacrifice needed to actually realize it. Warranted desperation is, in fact, righteously dangerous if it springs from an education about the abrogation of justice, fairness and opportunities for legitimate life chances.

Another tough assumption is that legitimately radical public spheres can spring forth stronger with schoolteacher collaboration, in a state with a recent history where the calculus of advertised, promoted civic value starts with a culture industry devoted to the

valorization of constant military and civilian police action, legiti-
mated violence, and repression of state "enemies," and support of
tin-pot police states from Los Angeles to Singapore, while ignoring
the legitimate military needs of less strategically important ports
of call. First, these are teachers who must themselves work out of
the engulfing web of cultural violence and living room electronic
target practice, with the centralized legitimation of winner-take-all
violence in professional sports. In short, hope must be developed
through and beyond the absolutely bewildering shape-shifting
kaleidoscope of image production, spectacular distractions from
and justification of unwarranted, unjustified suffering.

Another assumption is that "cultural politics" can be done in the
eclipse of a legitimate conventional public sphere, for all our
academic ablutions are threatened with irrelevance. The fifty-year
university collaboration with the antidemocratic wing of the
national security state is a little reminder that academic freedom
can mean a lot of things to an arms dealer. Thus, none of us are
immune to the relegation of our "cultural" politics to just that—a
role of "culture" as high-class leisure. In this case, it is a form of
leisure that academics engage in as part of the state's legitimation
of the language of free thought, of democracy, of overheated
radicalism percolating in university publishing "co-ops," while at
the other end of campus somebody is getting his or her fifteenth
grant for laser-guided missile research.

True hope is just that, a belief in something despite a slim
justification for it. I believe that it is all right to dedicate one's life
to the elucidation of conditions within which citizens must labor
to understand their chances for freedom, even if that is done in chains
of one sort or another. That is just simply an appeal to the dignity
of the human right to inquire and understand, and the requirement
that this is simply the precondition to anything like a reasoned
strategy for a jailbreak.

The contemporary dialogue regarding a language of possibility
has been based on the rejection of rigid analyses of power which
tended to eliminate the notion that dominant class interests are
vulnerable. Svi Shapiro has written that "social and educational

entitlements have been won not because of, but in spite of, dominant class interests . . . sustained through continued struggles of
working class and popular social movements."[3] Peter McLaren,
critical of the "gloom of reproduction theory," has also railed
against the classicism and spiritual poverty implicit in the work of
neoconservatives Hirsch and Bloom.[4] Henry Giroux has written,
citing the growing ethnographic literature on forms of student
resistance, that none of the "reproductionist approaches focus
adequately on the dynamic nature of the antagonistic relationships
that actually transpire at the day-to-day level of schooling." He
wants to develop "pedagogical practices that use the lived experiences of the students themselves as a starting point for developing
classroom experiences in which students discover how they give
meaning to the world and how such meaning can be used reflec-
tively to discover its own sources and limits."[5] He would locate
the heart of his pedagogy in an analysis of their own experience
and that of the culture around them. They would "study their own
class specific histories and interests" and analyze "the popular
culture that they use to express and confirm themselves."[6] Shapiro
celebrates the faith that schools are more than the mouthpieces of
capital, that a rigid functionalism is wrong, and that liberatory
pedagogy is one that helps students to "interrogate their inner
histories and experiences critically."[7] As extrapolations from
Gramsci, these arguments seem to be partially correct. Gramsci
does insist that pedagogy be creative and alive to the connections
teachers may draw between traditional academic work and the
lives of their students. Yet the "language of possibility" neglects
to emphasize Gramsci's belief that, while schooling must be
creative and alive, it must not degenerate into "self-involvement."

The possibility theorists' argument seeks analysis of inner "class
specific" histories, but is one that rejects the liberal studies that if
done properly, Gramsci argues, equip the intellect to make this
analysis more meaningful to the student. Henry Giroux has identified culture, as represented in the forms of academic structure, as
a complex of domination.[8] While he wants to move "beyond the
hollow space of enlightenment rationality," his critique appears,

contrary to his intent, to be a retreat back to a region in this "space" that is particularly devoid of possibility for the working-class student.[9] It would never be the intent of the possibility theorists to see their work result in a new form of the tracking they despise. However, if only privileged students are receiving a traditional, liberal education, a different education for working-class students, designed to "heal" meaning-starved general and "career" curricula, may not have the same power to effectively deliver educational capital.

The argument in this chapter evolves more from the strains of Left theory out of which the recent "possibility theorists" have drawn much of their argument.

Giroux may be right that reproduction theory "trapped in the theoretical cemetery of Orwellian pessimism" may be inadequate for the construction of an educational project.[10] It may be too simplified and overdetermined. Yet the arguments for increasing the "primacy of student experience" are not necessarily sufficient for what McLaren has called "political self-empowerment."[11] George Wood and Landon Beyer argued strenuously for schooling founded in participatory democracy, and emphasized political empowerment. They support the requirement for "equal access to requisite knowledge," upon which equal power must be based, and make a special effort to cite radical curriculum theorist Michael Apple's support for Adler's *Paidea*.[12] Wood and Beyer reassert a preoccupation with a pedagogy of "self-reflectivity," emphasizing knowledge upon which students' personal and political lives are based. Adler's *Paidea* notwithstanding, "dialectical" radical pedagogies threaten to retreat not wrongly but *prematurely* from knowledge structures that are the basis of requirements for intellectual power.

This chapter explores the potential pedagogy that is implied in each of the two sources from which the possibilitarians have drawn—from Gramsci and from Left theory of cultural revolution, particularly through Marcuse, and from several other sources from which critical educators may draw strength. Both strains share an understanding of the potential inherent in the prospect of cultural

revolution. The possibilitarians at their most perceptive have taken
into account the forms of pedagogy that are the logical outcome of
each of these strains: Gramsci's notions of classical education and
the "antipedagogy" of the most challenging group of cultural
revolutionaries, the surrealists. Finally there is a tradition of a
certain quietism regarding the ultimate goal of a life, a life which
centers on a search for enlightenment and a kind of salvation. We
enter this world for a brief time to explore contemplative traditions
as a source of strength in addition to the others discussed here,
strength which may be drawn upon as a form of resistance and a
source of legitimate hope.[13]

GRAMSCI: CONSCIOUSNESS
BY INTELLECTION

Gramsci's prescription for "counterhegemonic" education is not an
attack on academic pedagogy, but a celebration of it. For Gramsci,
it was axiomatic that liberatory intellection be "well informed from
the culture's stock of received truth." Factual knowledge will act
as scaffolding for the building of intellectual structures. The closest
Gramsci comes to a critique of intellectual banking is in his faith
that a "well-taught" liberal studies will motivate intellect intrinsi-
cally, and warnings, consistent to Freire's that a slavish attitude
toward fact collection as a source of status is counterproductive.
Gramsci writes, "the fact is that only by degrees, one stage at a
time, has humanity acquired consciousness of its own value and
won for itself the right to throw off the patterns of organization
imposed on it by minorities at a previous period in history. . . .
Every revolution has been preceded by an intense labor of criticism, by the diffusion of culture and the spread of ideas amongst
masses of men who are at first resistant, and think only of solving
their own immediate economic and political problems for themselves, who have no ties of solidarity with others in the same
condition."[14] Gramsci here appears not only to insist on "furnishing"
the mind, but to warn against a self-involved pedagogy.

For Gramsci, critique "implies culture" and "consciousness of a self which is opposed to others, which is differentiated and, once having set itself a goal, can judge facts and events other than in themselves or for themselves but also insofar as they tend to drive history forward or backward. To know oneself, to free oneself from a state of chaos, is to exist as an element of order—but of one's own order and one's own discipline in striving for an ideal. And we cannot be successful in this unless we also know others, their history, the successive efforts they have made to be what they are, to create the civilization they have created and which we seek to replace with our own. In other words, we must form some idea of nature and its laws in order to come to know the laws governing the mind."[15] Gramsci is intensely insistent that it is the intellect and the awareness of the teacher who "must be . . . conscious of his obligation to accelerate and regulate the child's formation in conformity with the former and in conflict with the latter."[16] His insistence on the importance of the teacher strengthens his resolve for a traditional curriculum. For this demands that teachers must be strong enough to teach this material, or if they are weak, may be less able to stand in its way, due to the power of the material.[17] He argues for Latin and Greek, and schooling that is "formal," not having "immediate or too immediate practical purposes. It must be formative, while being 'instructive'—in other words rich in concrete facts."[18] Gramsci enjoined working-class "organic intellectuals," upon whom the drive towards working-class hegemony would be based, to learn to submit their thought to the discipline of the written word. Only through the mastery of print could their thinking gain the precision necessary to engage in debate with intellectuals who were the products of an orthodox higher education and to communicate with their fellow workers.[19]

One problem appears to be the way Gramsci's theme of the vulnerability and "cultural" dimensions of ideological hegemony have been employed to imply a "terrain" of struggle that, according to the possibilitarians, the reproduction theorists have not seen. While this terrain may be legitimate, it is wrong to imply, as several of the possibility theorists have done, that it is best done as part of a pedagogy associated, for example, with Freire's critique of "banking education." In fact, all the evidence suggests that Gramsci argued this "terrain" can only be held by intellectuals, schooled in the habit, discipline, and rigor of "liberal education." Gramsci insisted on the development of rational faculties and stores of "facts." He argued for traditional notions of intellectual power, rationally applied, equipping the "organic" intellectual. Gramsci did not want "lived experiences" included for their own sake. Nor did he believe that this process of "interrogation" is, by itself, a means to enlightenment. He wanted lived experiences to give meaning to the traditional texts and their historical meanings.

To take Gramsci seriously is to seriously consider the pedagogy he recommends. We must see that the terrain of working-class possibility may be argued to center squarely on the effort to equip working-class children with the linguistic and cultural power contained in the power codes of traditional academic studies. Given the structure of public schooling, holding schools to equitably deliver on this promise may in fact be the *only* form of possibility we may purchase for the marginalized school child.

Giroux in particular has grappled with the Gramscian legacy with interesting, if at times ambiguous, results. His vigorous critique of Entwistle's apology for Gramsci's pedagogical conservatism is a powerful indictment of this alliance of traditional education with possibilities for radical education.[20] He argues that Entwistle toadys to neoconservative, antiprogressive pedagogues like Ravitch, by offering to support an outline of their reactionary curriculum as a preparation for radical intellectuals. This is, in effect, like putting William Bennett in cahoots with Gramsci.

Whatever the effect of Entwistle, alliance with the antidemocratic, privilege protecting impulses of neoconservative pedagogy and schooling is self-defeating. When traditional pedagogy is exploited as a coded practice working to accelerate working-class flight from and failure in the credentials competition, it is deeply antidemocratic. Yet, in its best context and application, liberal education contains forms of possibility that can offer working-class students the intellectual tools with which to fashion a critical consciousness. While Giroux warned that conservative pedagogy

offered *only* habit and inculcation, Gramsci implied an education
where habit was not an end in itself but a means of enlightened
discipline toward liberating intellection.[21] This effort to build
intellect also offered a palliative to the neoprogressive "life adjustment" education which stripped many working-class students of
their right to the tools of intellect and had "betrayed the interests
of the poor and minorities who desperately needed to learn how to
read, write, and calculate."[22]

We are left with the suggestion for a curriculum that jettisons
the worst examples of what came to be called progressive education. Gramsci's effort to give an elite education to working-class
children cannot be tainted with the ceremonialism of high-class
matriculation, where feigned scholarship triggers a rite of passage
to the next level of status opportunity. If the effort is to "inculcate
the habit of scholarship among ordinary people" Gramsci wanted
to find a school form that would enable children of the subaltern
classes to achieve not only what ruling class students learned in
earlier times, but also to appropriate critically the best dimensions
of their own histories, experiences and culture.[23]

What was and is required is an education that enables more
students to meaningfully "contest the moral and intellectual leadership of society by entering the public sphere of both institutional
and political life where people debated their truths about education,
morality, and law."[24] With Gramsci, "the task is to *appropriate*
critically those best features of traditional education practice,
which constituted the pedagogy of the ruling and mandarin
classes."[25] The key here is the nature of that appropriation. The
best part of this would be a curriculum "steeped in the ethical and
political imperative of educating students to provide the moral
and intellectual leadership necessary to struggle for a qualitatively
better life for all."[26] This is the context in which any "canons of
liberal arts provide one basis for . . . mastery."[27]

One source for this commitment comes, in part, from the tradition
of progressive education, at least that part of the tradition that was
not appropriated by the liberal education establishment for the
better "adjustment" of working-class students to their proper place

in the political economic order. Giroux and Aronowitz have in fact argued that this appropriation prepared the ground for the victory of the Right during the 1980s, and argued further that progressive education's participation in some facets of liberal educational humanism retains the best hope for a democratic education.

In his classic work, *Growing Up Absurd*, Paul Goodman, in 1960, articulated with prescient accuracy some of both the promise and possibility of progressive education. It is fitting that this work was the kind of existential meditation on the purpose of growing to personhood, which is now so out of fashion. It is an extended look at the dangers of an education designed for the molding of children as instruments fit for production, as commodities on the labor trading block. Fittingly Goodman was writing in reaction to the last great paroxysm of education reform that followed *Sputnik* in the heart of the cold war.

Goodman beautifully articulated a curriculum approach, with appropriate cautionaries. He begins with praise of the utopian impulse imbedded in the less instrumental, pragmatist progressive ideology. He praises the progressive temper and its effect on curriculum practice, especially as it emphasized its heritage in a history of civic radicalism, concentrating on problems of the wider society and equipping students with the means to identify as well as solve those. He praises the emphasis on learning by participation and practice in self-rule. But the one missing element is a weakness in humanist traditions which, at their best, exercise the imagination and *inspire* in unpredictable ways. This is a curriculum with grandeur, "explosive playfulness," and "religious quiet" that "cannot vary with what is temporarily convenient for a bad society, the definition of bad society being one that is not educational."[28]

Yet, the optimism inherent in the American progressive tradition should be leavened by the sobriety and caution of the Frankfurt school, and the aesthetic rationality implied by surrealism, for at the surface, "in the closed universe of instrumental rationality the emancipatory potentials of education are virtually hidden."[29] Indeed surrealism implies that so much consciousness lies beneath our awareness and offers a possibility through its aesthetic that there may be a relationship possible between the "progressivism" of Gramsci, the Frankfurt school's suspicion of rationality, and the radical antifoundationalism of the postmodern sensibility. Indeed, the "logic" of art finds its way into the heart of any interpretation. Forms of rationality competent to withstand the mystifications of instrumental capitalist saturation are found in the aesthetic rationality of art. This, at least for Adorno, was the only possible model for the organization and the rationality of the emancipated society.[30]

Yet, any aesthetic rationality is itself endangered by the capitalist saturation of both popular culture and elite art markets. The convulsive, emancipatory, liberatory value of poetry and art is inherent in its ability to mobilize the compassion at the base of all values worth holding. Neither Gramsci's traditionalism nor the entirety of cultural revolutionary art is adequate to a complete project for liberatory pedagogy in a world where myths of reform clutter our coherent awareness of the problems at hand for critical educators. Yet, each points to elements of Goodman's prescription for a distillation of the best of progressivism, allied with those liberal arts, and artistic and contemplative traditions which supply the "grandeur," the "explosive playfulness," and "the religious quiet" required for a purposeful, meaningful step toward legiti-mate, not ritual, emancipation. Antifoundationalism can be a sane part of a "distillation," which includes progressive rationality. These two sensibilities need not be mutually exclusive.

POWER AND CULTURAL REVOLUTION

Marcuse has argued that Gramsci, for all his faith in education, is skeptical about the possibility of cultural reform "without previous economic reform."[31] This would tend to ally Marcuse less with those who argue for a language of possibility than with a faith that creates a radical separation between educational practice and political-economic change. In addition, Gramsci's prescriptions appear counter to the skepticism, the lingering lack of faith in scientific rationality, which is an integral part of Left culture critique and which Marcuse represents. Marcuse has written, "today, what possible language, what possible image can crush and hypnotize minds and bodies which live in peaceful coexistence (and even profiting from) genocide, torture and poison." And, he states, violent images are the "daily equipment of mass media, sports, highways, places of recreation. They do not break the oppressive familiarity with destruction; they reproduce it."[32]

The Frankfurt school was generally concerned with the problem of subjectivity, consciousness, and culture and how these structures could operate in opposition to the Stalinist bureaucratic, instrumental edifice, and the entrenchment of European positivism. Marcuse noted the problem of the antirevolutionary working class and the paradox of the high stage of capitalist development coincident with their low stage of revolutionary potential. Citing the phenomena of surplus profits, welfarism, colonial labor, defense economy, he noted the power of consciousness as a revolutionary problem, and that "this class has much more to lose than its chains."[33] Marcuse is hinting at a problem of consciousness alteration that may not only be difficult to address from within a bourgeois institution, but to make that suggestion might simply be nonsense.

Giroux cites the work of Adorno and Horkheimer as sources for theory that locates the production of historical experience in the cultural realm.[34] He cites Marcuse as the prime mover of a theoretical position that argues that consciousness needs changing, yet he underplays Marcuse's emphasis on the enormity of the task. Following Marcuse he notes, "Depth psychology was needed, to explain the subjective dimension of liberation and domination. . . . Marx had relegated the psychic dimension to a secondary status."[35] Yet he has also noted the paradoxical nature of these writers and Marcuse for their paradoxical emphasis on the totality of cultural domination and a faith in the efficacy of human agency.[36] Giroux finds sustenance in this work for his resistance to a reproductionist critique that says that any struggle must be a species of false consciousness; a struggle ignores "clear" forms of collective empowerment.[37] It is one thing to locate a terrain in the cultural dimension of ideology. It is another to suggest a method for attacking the "fortress" of intellect.

Possibility theorists have begun to recognize the traditions of Left culture-critique, which is clear on the power required to dismantle the fortress of consciousness. Henry Giroux has, for example, described the power of artist Leon Golub and the way his aesthetic is bound to political opposition. In *Border Crossings: Cultural Workers and the Politics of Education*, Giroux takes the opportunity to expound the notion of popular culture and political opposition in terms that incorporate the power of art and cultural action. In *Disturbing Pleasures: Learning Popular Culture*, Giroux takes on the privileged presence of mass advertising and global cultural Disneyfication, and comments on these phenomena as part of a more complicated structure of consciousness formation to which critical educators must attend. Possibility theorists must continue acknowledging that the roots of this critique are grounded in one tradition that challenges directly any claim that this process may come exclusively or primarily from within a bourgeois institution. Somewhere, and if only to acknowledge Marcuse's allegiance to this position, the possibility theorists must consider that most radical challenge to institutional culture change, surrealism.

A PEDAGOGY FROM THE SURREAL

The surrealists were the archcultural revolutionaries of twentieth-century Left theory. The surrealist movement has made a powerful, coherent (one might argue incoherent) attempt to fight the fire of bourgeois rationality with water. This strain of the Left critique, which, while very different than Gramsci's pedagogy, is important as a reminder of the limitations inherent in the power of *either* didactic or dialectic rationality to effect meaningful liberatory education.

While popularly understood as a "school" of art and poetry, surrealism is best understood as a powerful political and artistic project dedicated to an argument that says institutional forms of educational change are nonsense, since it is institutional structure itself that contributes to and conditions the "immiseration" and madness of modern life. They see answers only in such extra-curricular activities as love, madness, intoxication, automatic writing, hypnotism, dreams, moments of "objective chance," and in vis-gammapropylethylamine, a non-narcotic drug. It is important to understand that Marcuse, to whom Giroux in particular refers as a guide toward an appropriate and sufficient theory of cultural revolution, was in support of the surrealist project.

The surrealist prescription is a "healing" education, revelatory, and therefore, radically emancipatory. The "language of possibility" is, for surrealist artists like Breton or Artaud, the screams and muttering anguish of the mad. Indeed, some of its "researches" might be just the kind of education required for smooth transition from school to the urban postindustrial world—for example, "the popular surrealist practice of riding an unattractive suburban train all day to nowhere and back again."[38] All humor aside (yet humor is central to the surrealist project), the coherence of this project, like the coherence of Gramsci's pedagogy, is that it faces the intensity of bourgeois consciousness squarely and challenges it with praxis that is only equally intense in response to the task. The surrealist program is a complex and radical effort to address the deep problem of bourgeois consciousness change. Marcuse's sympathy with this tradition led him to realize that the educational project must deal with the "catastrophe of human essence."[39] For him, cultural revolution is required to confront a "new type of capitalism which has universalized alienation."[40] He quotes surrealist poet-playwright Antonin Artaud, in support of an art with power to transform—"theater must leave the stage and go to the street. It must *shock*, cruelly shock and shatter the complacent consciousness."[41]

Bruce Brown has noted the important role played by surrealist theory in the development of the New Left challenge to consciousness. He argues that the power of consciousness was the concern for those shocked by the developments of the twentieth century.[42] He hints at the "political (Debsian)" Marxists' distrust of culture and sexuality. This concern may be applied to the possibility theorist's resistance to tangentially pedagogical forms of intellection.[43] The work of Freud has a central place in Frankfurt school theory, yet the possibility theorists are quiet regarding the implications of Freudian critique implicit in neo-Marxist, New Left critique. Orthodox Freudianism was criticized for its power to justify repression. Orthodox Freudianism, like orthodox Marxism, resists the fluidity of consciousness.[44] Murray Bookchin commented on the growing separation between the cultural Left from the political Left. This perhaps explains why radical educational discourse appears unclear regarding its position on the power of consciousness and somewhat facile regarding the possibility for institutional counterhegemonic education.[45]

For the surrealists, the working class is "suffused with a fear sown by the ruling class, and afflicted by bourgeois illusions, religious superstition and sexual anxieties" to the degree that consciousness becomes a fortress of mystification. To this must be addressed a healing, sometimes a shocking, project of radical transformation.[46]

Franklin Rosemont clarifies a potential misunderstanding that derives from the popular notion of the surrealist movement. He writes, "Contrary to prevalent mis-definitions, surrealism is not an aesthetic doctrine, nor a philosophical system, nor a mere literary or artistic school. It is an unrelenting revolt against a civilization that reduces all human aspirations to market values, religious impostures, universal boredom and misery."[47] The surrealists sensed that nonrationality was the force animating twentieth-century Europe below the surface of traditional art, philosophy, and science. "Surreality" is intensely concentrated truth beyond rationality. Not a "deconstruction" of text or reality, surrealism expresses a faith that truth is possible even though it is buried beneath the crust of bourgeois convention. In this respect, surrealists differ dramatically from the aesthetic school that preceded them and with which they are often confused—Dada. Without the Dada movement, surrealism cannot be fully understood, but the surrealists differed in the meaning of their project. Both "Dada and Surrealism were born out of the artist's awareness of a society gone haywire and clinging to rational explanations of increasingly irrational twentieth-century experiences."[48] However, Dada refused to enter the fray and become committed to a reconstitutive political project. Dadaists remained aloof from human suffering, seemingly detached from the plight of the human spirit which made meaningful the madness and whimsy of their art. Dada's concern with humanity might be summed up in a quote by artist Francis Picabia, who wanted us to know that, "vegetables are more serious than men and more sensitive to frost."[49]

Surrealism arose in Paris after the First World War, and later became an international movement. It is represented in spirit no better than through the writing and art of André Breton. Breton was the molten core of surrealism and its most articulate spokesperson regarding the social-revolutionary project to which surrealism would respond. Breton's concerns appear sympathetic to those of later writers, such as Marcuse, concerned with cultural revolution, and unsatisfied with "bourgeois despotic Reason, which barely conceals the capitalist's malevolent leer . . . (as well as the) bureaucratic mysticism exemplified by the Stalinists' petrified dialectic."[50]

Artaud, madman and poet of the movement, writes "logical Europe endlessly crushes the mind between the jaws of two extremes. It opens and recloses the mind . . . our writers, our thinkers, our doctors, our dunces, are agreed to fail in life."[51]

The crucial difference between the political and cultural Left might be stated epigrammatically. Transform the world, said Marx. *Change Life*, said the proto-surrealist Rimbaud.[52] For Breton and the surrealists this change required forms of intellect that run counter to traditional prescriptions for academic reform. In many respects thought, rational thought itself, becomes "antilife," and reason itself is seen as corrupted by society and its educational system.[53] In "Revolution Now and Forever" Breton drove home the theme of structural corruption. He wrote, "wherever Western civilization is dominant all human contact has disappeared, except contact from which money can be made."[54]

The totality of this critique is reinforced by the themes that appear dominant in the surrealist program. A key element in surrealism is the place of love and passion as a route to liberatory intellection. Like Reich, the surrealists saw revolutionary power in love—"mad love"—which would reveal, by its juxtaposition to repressive structures, the "crisis of everyday life."[55]

There are a variety of other themes in the surrealist preoccupation that appear to be decidedly counterpedagogical. Violence, fascination with "objective chance," dreams, drugs, hypnotism, automatism, and other extreme states, these characterize the program of the surrealists. These states and activities leading to them are part of a faith, a faith that has human emancipation "the only cause worth serving," at its heart.[56] The surrealists were deeply suspicious of institutional and political means of change in the modern world, yet their "artistic" program was maintained as a method of achieving social revolutionary change. The surrealists, "having experienced little but deception in their attempts to change our way of life and to transform the world by militant political means . . . rather than accept a myth not of their own making . . . determined to refurbish one with deep roots in poetry and the world of dreams, the twin realms of language and desire."[57]

What characterizes the surrealist project is total suspicion of institutional forms of consciousness change. Yet the power of this suspicion is matched by an absolute faith in their own methods, which they argue "give a scientific basis into the mutation and origin of ideological images."[58] For all their skepticism, they reflect great hope that each of their "researches" may work to "liberate humanity from the ideological shackles that enforce the contradiction between dream and waking life."[59]

The explosiveness and improvisatory nature of surrealist activity might lead one to conclude that it is random, even meaningless. Indeed, a significant part of their practice consists of a descent into the unconscious. For example, the techniques of automatism, automatic writing, and painting are not simply a random clash of images. The power of these "random" juxtapositions of images lies not in whimsy, in their ability to delight, but in the shocking and mythic power of poetic analogy and incantation. Convulsive beauty, objective chance, critical paranoia, games, "inquiries," and vis-gammapropylethylamine were the first concrete steps in the "ultimate liquidation of all debilitating remnants of Greco-Roman, Christian bourgeois, Cartesian/positivist heritage."[60] This is not the stuff of sophomore U.S. history.

Surrealist activity is the quintessential antipedagogy, yet, for Breton and the surrealists, it is the ultimate and only means of addressing the twin fortresses of consciousness supporting bourgeois capitalist degradation and Stalinist repression and bureaucracy. Breton believed that no political program may stand in the way of this project. His faith in Marx, allegiance to Trotsky, and hatred of Stalinism are well documented. Yet, for Breton, no Marxist practice may interfere with art. In Mexico, he met with Trotsky, and drafted with him the manifesto "For the Independence of Revolutionary Art." He founded, with painter Diego Rivera, the International Federation of Independent Revolutionary Artists (FIARI), committed to these principles. "What we want is . . . the independence of art for the revolution, the revolution, for the definitive liberation of art."[61]

The argument here is not meant mainly to be an explication of aesthetic theory. It is, rather, an effort to illuminate the requirements of consciousness transformation demanded by the archetypal cultural revolutionaries on the Left. For them, language is not a means of knowing but a means of forgetting. The anarchy of automatism, dreams, intoxication, are clearly not the stuff of contemporary Left institutional pedagogy. Yet, this stuff of dreams is the route, for the surrealist Left critique, to any "possibility" of liberatory intellection. A surrealist antipedagogy is an attempt to break the edifice of conscious collaboration with structures of oppression. Richard Brosio has called the possibilitarians "motivational theorists."[62] For surrealists it is naive to believe in motivational possibility emerging without an explosive psychic event. The crust of bourgeois convention is too thick to permit radical strip mining without first blasting away the "overburden."

CONCLUSION

This chapter is not a reconciliation of Gramsci's traditionalism with the antipedagogy of surrealism. Indeed, mutual consideration of these positions is as close as one can get to an educational dialectic between reason and chaos. Yet, if these lessons are meaningful, consciousness change may not take place if either traditional forms of intellect or passionate search for enlightenment is lacking. My purpose has been to explore two direct influences in Left theory from which the possibilitarians have, directly or indirectly, drawn strength.

I believe there is rich suggestion in each for a realistic interpretation of possibility as a language of hope after Bowles and Gintis and the nuclear winter of reproductionism. But the lesson of both Gramsci's pedagogy and the surrealist antipedagogy must be kept squarely in mind. Gramsci's pedagogy reminds us that we must not let up on the struggle to win for marginalized and working-class children the right to the class codes and skills that the privileged pass on to their own. A lack of commitment to this goal leaves any theorist of possibility open to a more insidious possibility— development of anti-intellectuals who know not enough, nor how to, demand more of the world.

Well-intentioned concern for social justice has led these writers to emphasize "critical literacy," yet to reject, if only by omission, explicit reference to an education that has forged the intellects of our civilization's most literate critics, including, I suspect, the intellects of the possibilitarians themselves. They have perhaps rightly indicted the reproduction theorists for using theory to explain away the schools' failure to alleviate suffering.

Any "counterhegemonic" education that would disavow the important parts of a traditional pedagogy would make the same mistake as reproductionism. It would allow, in practice if not in theory, anyone to excuse public schools for those entombed there in their illiteracy.

The examples of radical scholarship mentioned here point to a need for caution and perhaps redirection on the part of those with a concern for liberatory education. It is wrong, if Gramsci is right, to ignore or undervalue the rigor required to master the codes of privilege and the intellectual power conferred by a creative approach to, and an immersion in, the liberal studies. It is wrong, if the surrealists are right, to argue that the project of consciousness alteration is anything but immense and not best addressed directly or initially from within any institution. In either case the possibilitarians should consider these unsettling portions of two traditions from which they themselves, directly or indirectly, have tried to construct a language of hope for the liberation of intellect and consciousness.

NOTES

1. From Gramsci, "Observations on the School: In Search of the Educational Principle," in David Forgacs, ed., *An Antonio Gramsci Reader, Selected Writings: 1916–1935* (New York: Schocken Books, 1988), p. 315.

2. From Jean Cocteau's film *Wedding on the Eiffel Tower*, quoted in Nahma Sandrow, *Surrealism: Theater Arts and Ideas* (New York: Harper and Row, 1972), p. 94.

3. Svi Shapiro, "Beyond the Sociology of Education: Culture, Politics and the Promise of Educational Change," *Educational Theory* 38, no. 4 (Fall 1988): 421.

4. Peter McLaren, *Life in Schools* (New York: Longman, 1989), pp. 20, 200.

5. Henry Giroux, *Ideology, Culture and the Process of Schooling* (Philadelphia: Temple University Press, 1981), p. 29.

6. Ibid., p. 31.

7. Shapiro, "Beyond the Sociology," p. 421.

8. Giroux, *Ideology*, p. 26.

9. Henry Giroux, *Theory and Resistance in Education: A Pedagogy for the Opposition* (South Hadley, Mass.: Bergin & Garvey, 1983), p. 209.

10. Ibid., p. 108.

11. McLaren, *Life in Schools*, pp. 189, 197.

12. Landon Beyer and George H. Wood, "Critical Inquiry and Moral Action in Education," *Educational Theory* 36, no. 1 (Winter 1986): 9–12.

13. Giroux, *Theory and Resistance*, pp. 22–25.

14. David Forgacs, ed., *Gramsci Reader*, p. 58.

15. Ibid.

16. Ibid., p. 313.

17. Ibid., p. 316.

18. Ibid., p. 317.

19. Harold Entwistle, *Class, Culture and Education* (Cambridge: Methuen, 1978), p. 98. Elsewhere, David Forgacs has argued that Gramsci's traditionalism can be explained due to his experience as a "scholarship boy" in Sardinia. Naturally his early education influenced his pedagogical thought. His faith in intellectual rigor should not be explained away by his early experience. It is more logical to conclude that Gramsci valued his education as an integral part of his growth as a radical intellectual. (See Forgacs, *Gramsci Reader*, p. 55.)

20. Henry Giroux, review of Harold Entwistle, *Antonio Gramsci: Conservative Schooling for Radical Politics* (Boston: Routledge & Kegan Paul, 1979) in *Telos* 45 (Fall 1980): 215–224.

21. Stanley Aronowitz and Henry A. Giroux, *Education under Siege* (South Hadley, Mass.: Bergin & Garvey, 1986), p. 9. In *Education Still under Siege* (Westport, Conn.: Bergin & Garvey, 1993), Aronowitz and Giroux acknowledge that classics in the liberal studies tradition, such as Plato's *Republic*, if used with a hermeneutic approach and appropriated by public schoolchildren, could be incorporated as part of the logic of a curriculum for possibility, providing this process results in their decanonization (p. 154).

22. Ibid.

23. Ibid., p. 11.

24. Ibid.

25. Ibid.

26. Ibid., p. 141.

27. Ibid.

28. Paul Goodman, *Growing Up Absurd* (New York: Random House, 1960), p. 83.

29. Albrecht Wellmer, "Reason, Utopia and the Dialectic of Enlightenment," in Richard J. Bernstein, ed., *Habermas and Modernity* (Cambridge: MIT Press, 1985), p. 49.

30. Ibid.

31. Herbert Marcuse, *Counterrevolution and Revolt* (Boston: Beacon Press, 1972), p. 161.

32. Marcuse, *Counterrevolution and Revolt*, p. 112.

33. Ibid., p. 5.

34. Giroux, *Theory and Resistance*, p. 23.

35. Giroux, *Theory and Resistance*, pp. 27–28. Elsewhere he argues for Marcuse's specific contribution to the argument for an escape from an overdetermined reproductionism to a notion of resistance. See Giroux, "Theories of Reproduction and Resistance in the New Sociology of Education: A Critical Analysis," *Harvard Educational Review* 53, no. 3 (August 1883): 290.

36. Giroux, *Theory and Resistance*, p. 39.

37. Henry Giroux, *Schooling and the Struggle for Public Life: Critical Pedagogy in the Modern Age* (University of Minnesota Press, 1988), p. 206.

38. Sandrow, *Surrealism*, p. 27.

39. Bruce Brown, *Marx, Freud, and the Critique of Everyday Life* (London: Monthly Review Press, 1973), p. 9.

40. Ibid.

41. Marcuse, *Counterrevolution and Revolt*, p. 112.

42. Brown, *Marx, Freud*, p. 16.

43. Ibid., p. 17. Brown quotes Ernst Bloch, who in 1931 warned the "vulgar Marxists [who were] not keeping watch on what is happening to primitive and utopian trends. The Nazis are already occupying this territory and it will be an important one."

44. Ibid., p. 44.

45. Ibid., pp. 29–30.

46. Franklin Rosemont, ed., *André Breton* (New York: Monad, 1978), p. 69.

47. Ibid., p. 1.

48. Ibid., 95.

49. Ibid., p. 16.

50. Ibid., p. 46.

51. Patrick Waldberg, *Surrealism* (New York: Oxford University Press, 1965), p. 60.

52. Brown, *Marx, Freud*, p. 23.

53. Herbert S. Gershman, *The Surrealist Revolution in France* (Ann Arbor: University of Michigan Press, 1969), p. 16.

54. Rosemont, *André Breton*, p. 318.

55. Brown, *Marx, Freud*, p. 25. An example of this faith is evident, for example, in the program notes to Buñuel's "L'Age d'Or," which contain a statement that was signed by the leaders of the surrealist movement in Paris: Aragon, Breton, Crevel, Dali, Eluard, Peret, Tzara, et al. "The day will come when we realize that the very cornerstone of that violent liberation which reaches out for a cleaner life in the heart of the technological age that corrupts our cities is LOVE." In Sandrow, *Surrealism*, p. 29.

56. Rosemont, *André Breton*, p. 5.

57. Gershman, *Surrealist Revolution*, p. 4.

58. Rosemont, *André Breton*, p. 147.

59. Ibid., pp. 20–21. Breton's intention is mirrored in the experimental novel-like work *Nadja*. Even its title, the central character's name, is the beginning (but only the beginning!) of the Russian word for hope and is an expression of possibility. Yet, this is a possibility that lies outside institutional experience. See André Breton, *Nadja* (New York: Grove Press, 1960), p. 69.

60. Rosemont, *André Breton*, p. 71.

61. Gershman, *Surrealist Revolution*, p. 102. See also Waldberg, *Surrealism*, p. 18.

62. Richard Brosio, *The Frankfurt School: An Analysis of the Contradictions and Guises of Liberal Capitalist Societies*, Monograph 29, Muncie, Ind., Ball State University, 1980, p. 79.

6

Conclusion:
Symbols of Emancipation
and the Cargo Cult
of Education Reform

This book is a disquisition on the barbarity of institutional education reform. It has been developed in communication with the
critical theoretical tradition, and attempts an analysis of a broad
selection of phenomena, each of which throws light on the limits
of education discourse. This book has also been written with
respect to and by means of the conscious application of improvisatory surrealist technique. Disparate subjects and objects have
been forced together, fissionable material for the expansion of our
perception of realities hidden by the crust of reform rhetoric. The
language of education reform, when it undergoes such analysis,
exhibits effects contradictory to its rhetoric. While these effects
are numerous, they are characterized by an allegiance to the
promise of intellectual emancipation.

Critics of education from different parts of the political dialogue
have shared a unique disposition to see emancipation as a fundamental of educative experience. This is a rehabilitative illusion,
which functions to valorize various forms of education, and works
to camouflage the collaborative function of school reform—a
function closely allied to the resource and labor management
functions of capital. The geography of the ideological terrain of

emancipation is so ambiguous that its mapping must be the first object towards which a genuinely emancipatory theory and practice of pedagogy must be directed.

Mainstream education reform correctives competed for public media space in the 1980s, each offering its own vision of problem and solution. A full catalogue of the players is unnecessary, but for one example, Hirsch and Bloom saw reform in a renaissance of reason by the salvage of great Western concepts. They argued for a more truly rational appraisal of the possibilities of ratiocination, coming from the academy of teachers, in a world of fragmented consciousness cohabited paradoxically by forms of image starvation and satiation, and the electronic flotsam of what Gary Snyder called high-quantity, low-quality information. All of the academic conservatives harkened back to the transporting power of classical forms of education without much thought regarding a meaningful delivery system during a time when their allies in politics were gutting the launch facilities of public education, to be replaced with the launch pads of defense hardware, shuttle satellite delivery systems, laser-guided strategic delivery systems, and other key hardware for the security state.

Jonathan Kozol's hectoring from the middle, while it reminded us of a more romantic age, where he and Paul Goodman, for example, might be taken seriously, bounced from his bitter books to the talk show, book-signing circuit, and like a flat rock thrown well on a smooth lake made a small ripple before sinking. Kozol was right to hate the inequality of schooling outcomes, but was mistaken not to focus on the distractions of social power that legitimate what these crumbling schools advertise—that "rat-holes" are still a bad investment, except that they do well to circulate a vision of deviance against which we should turn our domestic attention, and a further argument for global "reinvestment" in human and material capital.[1]

The attacks of both Left liberals like Kozol and the conservative savaging of Hirsch, Bloom, and Bennett were equally equilibrating forces and can be reminders of what we could easily forget, that education may in some sense fail usefully with or without honor.

This failure serves to bolster consciousness fragmentation, decreasing powers of concentration, and distraction upon which an edifice of consumption and political disorientation is built. The best critical educational theory on the Left, while correcting appropriately for the doom-saying of orthodox reproduction theory and superstructural domination of education, must continue to grapple more vigorously with the need for curriculum and practice to deal with clearing the obstacles of distraction, simulation, and continuance of a growing confusion within what is left of a traditional public sphere. The implosion of emancipatory possibility in the global Disneyfication of politics and capital is a problem of underestimated enormity. The Left is also confronting a political black hole, where the "fall of communism" draws every impulse toward solidarity into its grip, rendering working-class identity, much less solidarity, quaint, if not obsolete.

This book is a meditation over a series of cases that demonstrate the depth of intellectual domestication required for our main myths of emancipation and upward educational mobility to work. It is an effort to grapple with some key signs and images of delusion that have proliferated in this culture. The key rhetorical devices of emancipation: excellence, technology, synthetic literacy, empowerment, appearing more as an organization of effects, each a revised talisman for the techno-feudal culture for capital that threatens to engulf possibilities for enlightenment and consciousness in this time.

It is also a reminder that as long as there is money to be made from cultivating the ignorance of working people, education in the best sense is going to be, for their children, a rarity. It is written in response to the discourse of reform that emerged in the 1980s with, I argue, big windows to its absurd interior. Many commentators have written of the problems and inadequacy of the reform years of the 1980s. My focus is on the way reform themes are consistent with the absurdity of the relationship between postindustrialism and democratic public education. There are some small themes of petty bureaucracy and insufficient efforts to address the continued and worsening plight of working-class children in late twentieth-century public education. It is a story of larger proportions that asks questions regarding the dreamscape that forms clouds of rhetorical hope that drift and dissipate over the official landscape. This is, I discover now after having completed the writing, a dreary little volume, one that offers little hope beyond the efficacy of individual perseverance. That in fact may be its only virtue, standing dwarfed in a crowd of thundering tracts offering no institutional solution to the tightening downward spiral of bureaucratic failure that characterizes education reform.

Much of the absurdity of the current reform climate comes due to a persuasive mystification of the labor process and that education designed for the consumption of future participants in the labor market. In her thoughtful meditation on central dilemmas of this age, Hannah Arendt concentrated on the precariousness of self-definition based on labor. While it is inescapable, it is also crucial that our thinking on the consequences of contemporary labor be precise. She warns of the dangers of vanity bound up in our concern with institution building. This vanity is a central component explanation as to why our institutions of education are continuously generating rhetoric which, to paraphrase André Breton, is a mouth moving in the service of capital. It is a vanity of pernicious political reward in the worst sense of the political. Unlike the Native Americans who theorize that we must act mindful of how our works might affect the seventh generation, official concern is to bolster the profile of American business during the latest aneurysm of the business cycle or the imbalance of trade. The immortality of our works in education are of little concern. We seem to be unconcerned with the futility of these efforts in pursuit of vainglory or a higher profile. The most recent participation of intellectuals and academics in their race to be relevant to our business crises has been recognition that the magnificent futility of vanity under current conditions has gone unnoticed. As Arendt writes, "public admiration, is something to be used and consumed, and status, as we would say today, fulfills one need as food fulfills another: public admiration is consumed by individual vanity as food is consumed by hunger."[2]

This book is a somewhat extended dissertation on the impact of reform rhetoric, particularly the labor preparation material. It is a discourse on the interwoven metaphoric significance of education reform. It takes place during a slump in the fortunes of academic Marxian analysis. Beginning with a reflection on Arendt's *The Human Condition*, it is comforting to read her words during an earlier downturn in the German's stock. Writing in 1951, her chapter on labor begins, "In the following chapter, Karl Marx will be criticized. This is unfortunate at a time when so many writers who once made their living by explicit or tacit borrowing from the great wealth of Marxian ideas and insights have decided to become professional anti-Marxists, in the process of which one of them even discovered that Karl Marx himself was unable to make a living."[3] There is no shortage of professional Marx bashing to the right and left of educational theory, so her comments are a comforting reminder of the cyclical nature of academic bibliotherapy.

LEAVING NO TRACE

Much of this book is about not making a living, or about dealing with students whose training allows them to make a living for someone other than themselves. As such, Arendt's great discussion of the nature of existence around the themes of labor, action, freedom, slavery, and the active life is a perfect stepping off place. The lives and discourse of teachers have been thoroughly absorbed in the effort to rehabilitate their students for labor. This is the great theme of this generation of reform discourse. Arendt reminds us of the purposes of labor that transcend work in a capitalist labor exchange. She talks about "the man-made world of things, the human artifice erected by *homo faber*, becomes a home for mortal men, whose stability will endure and outlast the ever-changing movement of their lives and actions, only insomuch as it transcends both the sheer functionalism of things produced for consumption and the sheer utility of objects produced for use. Life in its nonbiological sense, the span of time each man has between birth and death, manifests itself in action and speech, both of which share with life its essential futility. "The doing of great deeds and the speaking of great words" will leave no trace, no product that might endure after the moment of action and the spoken word has passed."[4] She reminds us of the purposes of speech and action that are conditioned by education. And we may consider the nagging requirement that in our educational discourse, we as teachers, are conditioned by the surveillance of the state to direct training in the service of economic motives that have more to do with the ongoing damage to our students' capacities than to their personal or community enrichment, and to damage control regarding the continuing failure of postindustrial capitalism to provide fair distribution of opportunity and decent human work. Enrichment is a state prerogative, and teachers are to be enlisted in the improvement of the sheer functionalism of things produced for consumption.

We have been called to turn our focus away from traditional reasons for dialogue, contemplation, and study—enlightenment, salvation, wisdom. Teachers in the climate of higher levels of state assessment and business-education "partnerships" are rewarded for forgetting the role of the teacher as a seasoned participant in the search for salvation, for enlightenment. Arendt's problem of the human condition suggests that educating has been purposely divorced from the process of judgment, the critique which would discuss whether we should be making objects and machines that are fit for men. Rather our "job" has become to make sure that men are fit for objects and machines.

Arendt argues that thought is possible wherever men live under conditions of political freedom. Indeed the conditions of "civilized" tyranny were of great concern to her. What must be considered is the role teaching may play in the creation or destruction of human capacities, now that these capacities have become severely truncated by their definition as functions of the economic, mechanical problems of the postindustrial labor market. Where political freedom has been overdefined as the ability to freely mobilize labor and commodities in a global market, civic, social, and personal goods in education are reshaped to conform to these forces. Schooling becomes a simulation of a host of historic and metaphoric signifiers advanced to rationalize the truncation of working-class chances, while obscuring the possibilities for working-class consciousness.

Arendt places in our view the challenge that we might mediate the argument for a connection between alienated labor and education. She quotes Cato: "Never is he more active than when he does nothing, never is he less alone than when he is by himself."[5] The suggestion here is that as a work in himself, man is complete also in contemplation, in solitude, perhaps more so than when nagged by his fit for the unfree service of others, other purposes, other profits, other definitions of correct attitude and action, at the heart of alienated labor.

Part of the argument of this book is that critical educators must be more vigilantly aware of the role working-class ignorance and distraction play in the generation of ruling-class profits. Participants in schooling cannot underestimate the value of distraction, forgetting, and unconsciousness in the inability of laboring classes to compete for available circulating surplus value. School reform and reform dialogue in general is the best place to find concentrated evidence of these values, in much the same way that a kennel club show is a showcase for manufactured canine virtue, the vanity of owners. Reform is a critical showcase of ruling opinion, a place for "cutting edge" researchers, pundits, and politicians to offer and distribute their wares.

Arendt discusses the blurring of the state and family and the distinction between public and private realms which, she argues, existed at least from the rise of the city-state. Contrasted to the possibilities arising from this dichotomy is the rise of the "social," a construction with roots not in the local but in the "public" realm of the nation state. This emergence has blurred the public/private distinction, resulting in a consciousness that removes the heart of meaning from both public and private realms. "In our understanding," she writes, "the dividing line is entirely blurred, because we see the body of peoples and political communities in the image of a family whose everyday affairs have to be taken care of by a gigantic, nation-wide administration of housekeeping. The

scientific thought that corresponds to this development is no longer
political science but 'national economy' or 'social economy' or
Volkswirtschaft, all of which indicate a kind of 'collective housekeeping.' "[6] In a real sense, education reform in our time must be
an extension of social housekeeping, a social appropriation of the
private goods for social utility. Privacy and the individual and the
true sense of the public interest as a living democratic extension
are crippled. As education connects to the public good, contemplation and philosophy, both emerging in a private or nearly
private realm, are likewise crippled in the service of the socialized
economic interest, "as seen on TV." The ancient gulf between
private and public has disappeared into the mediated netherworld
of the social, constructed around images and myths of advertised
exchange value, as Warhol circumscribed it, where everything is
a copy.

Thomas Merton reflected on the requirements of contemplation
and the purposes for human action and reminds us of the dilemma
that this new social dimension has delivered to us. He argues that
we come into this world for communion and self-transcendence—
for love—not to be a machine for other's use. While he argues that
we waste time modeling ourselves on the images presented to us
by an affluent marketing society, our state education officers are
pressing for students to be better formed as products, objects whose
character and judgment are to be evaluated for their utility as
efficient, competitive producers of use-value and consumers of
their own waste—shit eaters.[7]

In contrast, and in violation of the "social" use of education, for
Merton teaching is a form of love and of worship.[8] Man has ceased
being a person and by subsumption in the social becomes an
"individual." This individual is defined by the massive numerical
technical concept of man that destroys love by substituting the
individual for the person.[9] "We live in a world in which, though
we clutter it with our possessions, our projects, our exploitations,
and our machinery, we ourselves are absent."[10] Yet it is just to this
clutter that the focus of education reform has bowed in the last
ten years.

Merton's brilliant discussion of South Pacific cargo cults is an apt metaphor for the tenor of discussion at the center (and to the right) of recent reform. Cargo cults emerged in areas affected by the rapid and confusing changes wrought by Western colonialism in Southeast Asia, Africa, and particularly in the South Pacific Islands. For years after the coming of the white man, islanders heard their bosses talk about the coming of the cargo on delivery ships. "Kago" came to have a very important meaning for the natives. "Everything will be all right 'when the kago comes,' " the white man was saying. "When the kago comes we shall have pickles, and the cloth we need, and scissors, and the tobacco we are running out of. When the kago comes we shall have beer and whiskey and rice." The coming of the kago came to mean the goods associated with the white trader, the things that defined his difference from the native. The difference between native and colonial was not simply one involving race. Rather it "was the more radical distinction between those who could send for and receive cargo and those who never got any cargo of their own but depended on the white man for a rather miserable living. . . . For the native, to receive his own cargo "would mean readmission to the human race."[11]

Merton argued that we in the West live by similar sets of myths. One such myth is the relationship between education and the trappings of consumer and market success. The latest wave of reform has set a standard for the trappings of an education that might resemble the schooling found in those places "where the kago comes," like Japan and Germany. Until recent downturns in both of those economic "miracles," educators in the United States were being implored to retool schooling along Japanese lines, for example, longer school hours, higher standards, more rigorous examination, or as in Germany, with more rigorous efforts to vocationalize schooling with the incorporation of craft and trade education. These are among the numerous ways American educators were asked to reform schooling. The recent growth in national unemployment, political extremism, and dips in profitability in both of those beacons of educational success is perhaps a reminder of how tenuous are the arguments for economic and educational relationship.

Merton writes of the Yali cult that arose in New Guinea around the middle of this century. In this cult flowers played a part in the secret magic by which the whites obtained their cargo. White people liked to keep fresh-flower vases in the homes. Natives, seeing this and discussing its significance, began to decorate entire villages with enormous amounts of flowers in the thought that if they did this maybe cargo would come to them too.[12] A host of quasi-clerical academics have served as the spirit guides for the acceleration and sanctification of appropriate educational decorations: Bloom, and Bennett, Ravitch, Hirsch and Finn, and so forth. We have our prophets who have accelerated the frenzy. Our flower vases were, and remain, full. For one example, the National Commission on Excellence in Education (NCEE) offers a bouquet of "knowledge, learning, information and skilled intelligence." These are the "raw materials of international commerce and are today spreading throughout the world as vigorously as miracle drugs, synthetic fertilizers, and blue jeans did earlier. If only to keep and improve on the slim competitive edge we will retain in world markets, we must rededicate ourselves to the reform of our educational system."[13]

I would liken reform rhetoric to the same ineffective, desperate nature of Yali flowerpots. Decorative language about knowledge and skilled intelligence will not gloss over the fact that the kago will come, the productivity will increase, the extent to which working-class children here will be in competition for work with impoverished Pacific Rim labor for a place at the high-tech production table. Students who mimic "quality circles" and habituate themselves to information processing in their classes on "computers" act out a decorative ritual with scant evidence that any of it contributes to the development of their capacities for enlightenment, wisdom, judgment, or authentic emancipation. Indeed, Merton argued that the cargo cults did little other than bring the community together in a mass myth.[14] The national and state assessment frenzy is to rehabilitate teachers as counterparts to the shop-floor goons in the circuit-board industry or the surveillance experts, and accumulating assessments of productivity as diligently as "supervisors" in the high-tech world of the "techno-serf" measuring keystrokes and "customer interaction time." They will be rewarded for their own productivity as "classroom managers" who turn out a salable "product that industry wants."

As such the "crisis in productivity" as Shapiro comments will be ensured not by the developed wisdom of these children but by their availability as a "less lackadaisical, more disciplined work force, better prepared to accept long hours of labor, and less prone to tardiness and absenteeism . . . for the employees of schools as well as their students, as in industry, there was a common message—one which, in the name of higher productivity, insisted on the increased scrutiny of individual performance, a more thorough system of monitoring skill levels, and a more pervasive use of rankings in order to maximize output."[15]

We could also correctly conclude that worker productivity, as it remains largely a factor of wages and benefits versus productive hours will be helped by omitting any liberal education that might equip students from understanding their right to organize in their own interests. To give the metaphor a good drubbing, the flowers in these pots must be carefully selected varieties of "knowledge and attitudes" which do not attract the stinging bees of labor consciousness or agitation.

NO OFFICIALS

This book is an extended analysis of a group of paradoxes and some ways in which these manifest themselves as group myths for our consumption. Labor domestication is a key theme and takes its character from the way this domestication is at odds with reform rhetoric of excellence. Where labor socialization becomes a key ingredient in arguments for a renewed competitive stance, educational excellence becomes a reality not in the sense of an education for personal freedom or intellectual emancipation, rather as a species of training for proper postindustrial consumption and production characteristics.

Reform pedagogy pits labor domestication against intellectual emancipation, but this subaltern agenda is obscured in the parade of simulated school effects that serve to mask the true future for working-class students, a future where they must show up in the work hall with qualities appropriate for competition with their global counterparts. Competition is heightened, assessments are more rigorously state managed as monopoly markets in labor increasingly pit global working-class children against each other for places at the production table. Whether this competition is real or illusory is unimportant, for both the illusion and reality serve a purpose. The illusion of struggle allows further mystification of the structural in capital's inability to fairly distribute opportunity. Blaming failures on weaknesses in human labor capital solves political and ideological problems in one stroke, regardless of the truth.

Education reform elaborates the irony of its calls for increased competition and excellence in the service of mind improvement, while this corrosive competition is complicit in the production of mental excellence for the winners of the standardized state-normed assessments at the expense of mind damage for the losers. The paradox of education not as enlightenment, as equipping students, as Jefferson had said, to be able to see what will secure or endanger their freedom, but as an exercise in self-deception regarding their true interests.

This book has been organized around a story of two persons and a factory, each of which becomes an archetype in this analysis of the reform discourse of the 1980s. That each participates in a different kind of change related to postindustrial life is integral to the way in which their participation hypostatizes the essence of the simulatory character of reform in the 1980s. Deuk Koo Kim is the lonely Korean fighter whose death in the ring in 1983 came in the context of an opening "debate" about the health and safety of boxing. Christa McAuliffe is the teacher whose selection as the "teacher in space" led to her untimely death in the catastrophic *Challenger* explosion in 1986. Her death also came during the great education reform discussions of that time. These two are both victims of the propaganda, the violence, and the bureaucratic rationalization of corrosive social contests. They are both largely forgotten today due to the bureaucratic heartlessness and illusionary purposes of the institutions to which they fell victim. In a larger sense their stories are illuminatory regarding the less public fate of the working-class combatants and participants at the Hawthorne telephone works described later, their counterpart victims in the falsely celebratory spectacle of reform and concomitant adjustments in capital during our time.

This book is an effort to re-engage a critical debate regarding the enormously ironic but crucial role that deception, distraction, advertising, and propaganda play in the various ideologies of excellence and upward mobility and character development in education. It is an effort to show the need to reemphasize the danger that scholar/teachers run when they remain observers rather than participants in designing the purposes for public instruction. I believe the great themes of the ongoing mystification of actual working-class chances are magnified by these stories of reform. In her prologue to *The Human Condition*, Arendt begins with a reminder about the events unfolding in the postwar world. She begins with a discussion of space. Space, as Sun Ra put it, is the Place. We are playing out our dreams of escaping earthly bonds. We are at the pinnacle of our intoxication with technological salvation no more than when we seek the stars. It is perhaps the place where we can be distracted from the exhaustion of the planet wrought by earlier technologies. Indeed Christa McAuliffe's participation in the shuttle program inhabits this place of salvation, however far from the scholastic traditions of soul salvation in the antiquity of her teaching profession. It is no coincidence that both her death and the rehabilitation of our memory of its cause are tied up in human vanity and forgetting, the traditional enemies of the scholastic vocation. Like Socrates, she was destroyed by the enemies of her guild.

If we extend the metaphor, we can uncover the deeper violence at the heart of our space science. We can emerge with the same fuel for international political dominance that launched the space program in response to *Sputnik*. We can unearth the very corporeal desire for the power to deliver an efficient ballistic missile containing the nuclear knockout. The raw exercise of power is uncovered as a central theme in all this excellent knowledge. Competition as a national obsession emerges. No activity more than boxing embodies better the mythologies of struggle, victory, upward mobility, and character shaping at the heart of both sport and education. No sport is more representative of the raw atavism supposedly anathema to our slick postmodern society. Space and sport are two of our most important distractions and centers for the discourse of excellence. That we forget the violence embedded in both in the late twentieth century is crucial. The parting shot is a glance at what is left of work, that earthly preoccupation of educators and the corporeal answer to earthly salvation. The sanctity of work is central to the American democratic ethos, where its virtues, as free engagement, enable meaningful politics and a purposeful civil space reserved for those who labor as well as for those whose privilege allows leisure for civic participation. The story of the fate of the Hawthorne works embodies much that would emerge from a dialectic of technique and corporeal struggle, in the myths of space and sport of previous chapters. This book resolves as a mythography but one which I hope illuminates rather than further obscures the path for critical educators in the difficult time to come.

Nobody other than Paul Goodman, I think, has shed a clearer light on the evils of educating children to fit a bad society. As noted earlier, he presciently contemplated the problem of growing children in a quasi-affluent, quasi-democratic society. He wondered whether we confuse socialization with "growing up," and speculated that any society requiring socialization would need to be finished, perfect.[16] He expresses a painful and rare awareness of the still current truth that we must educate children well in a world where decent human work is disappearing at an alarming rate. Socialization would come to mean spending our productive years "doing what is no good."[17] This was written about post-industrialism, before *anybody* knew it was a "crisis" and at a time of relative full employment.

He wrote also about the overmaturity of the economy, when the teachers are struggling to preserve the elementary system when the economy no longer requires it and is stingy about paying for it.[18] It is rare to read something thirty-five years dated that is more true now than it was then. He also reflects the instrumentality of his, and our, generation of education reforms—by his critique of differentiated schooling—Conant's "great talent hunt." Schools follow the rhetoric of economic society, which is necessarily divorced from academic cultivation of the young of the attainment of important goals they can work toward for their own sake. Children are measured and fitted for some place in the economy, chopped down and slotted or neglected if slots are oversubscribed.[19]

In short, Goodman reflects on an economic order totally unable to reflect and/or act to create meaningful occupation where none exists. This is part of the "unpedagogic motive" of education, relieving the home, controlling delinquency, and keeping kids from competing for jobs. He discusses the paradox involved in preparing children for the kind of "democratic" society that does not need them in any meaningful sense.[20] Goodman's wisdom was to note how tenuous is any prospective alliance between legitimate educators and the prerogatives of an economic state that runs schools with "unpedagogic" motives.

Giroux and Aronowitz echo Goodman's concern, but in response to a reform spasm thirty-five years later. They decry the new conservative public philosophy which "abdicates its responsibility to ensure that public schools can function to enable students to experience a meaningful sense of personal and political liberty and to live a life in accordance with moral rules and principles."[21] They suggest a place for a humanist curriculum which may foster the development of such a moral conscience, a sense of what Marcuse had referred to as compassionate valuing. These values may be distilled from the arts and letters that have led in the direction toward human value and legitimate virtue. "They are the condition for acquiring critical thinking in a society where the old labor, socialist and radical public institutions that once provided these amenities have all but disappeared."[22]

They warn also of the power of ritual credentialism to subsume any curriculum or consciousness development. Schooling and its most radical intellectual potential can be quickly disarmed by the inability of the "one-dimensional" mind of students socialized to respond only to schooling, as an empty ritual that tells employers the applicant has endured passage.[23] The degree becomes a talisman, a ritual prerequisite only, a sign of social and occupational formation. Indeed signs that liberatory education works against the totalizing prerogatives of business management would *also* be a sign that the school failed to work—as a rite—and became educational, ironically counterproductive to its own interests!

Goodman bemoaned "the appropriation of schooling as a culling and training ground" for access to the shrinking pool of high-status work places, where children are bored and stultified with "no effort to increase the pool of ability and the public schools are used effectively as training grounds for the monopolies and the armed forces."[24] A nation at risk indeed.

I recently heard the following news from a conservative colleague who is also a good friend, one whom I can trust. He said that nobody, and certainly no academic in the Reagan administration, ever believed for a second that bad education was causing our economic "mediocrity," or that improving standards would do anything to help it. It was all a ploy to get schools turned around. If he is right, I feel better about this book but worse about the educational state. If he is wrong, I feel better about both. It is hard to get a win-win proposition from a neo- much less a paleo-conservative these days, as Japan drifts into its second year of high unemployment and the skinheads brought jackboots back in fashion around the European saloons again.

Merton argued that education was to help save souls, and in so doing save society.[25] Despite the theater of reform, whether in 1959 or in 1999, it appears the fundamental task of teachers should not vary. Saving souls is an easier job, at least for well-educated teachers, easier than saving the national share of the global marketplace. "For such an education," Merton wrote, "one receives no degree, one graduates by rising from the dead."[26] It is an intellectual place where one is no longer afraid (is less afraid?) of death, or poverty, or failure, where one cannot be kept in disguise by society. "Be anything, madman, drunk—but not a success."[27]

With Goodman, Merton would argue the danger that we substitute the individual, the numerical unit of labor, for the person and that we live passively, well educated, with our "possessions, our projects, our exploitations and our machinery, but we ourselves are absent."[28]

Teaching and learning then must learn to live with the distractions, the spectacles and the ritual, yet must reinforce that we "come into the world for communion and self-transcendence—for love—not to be a machine for use."[29] True teaching and the compassionate valuing it implies must be a form of love and a form of worship, an antidote to the obliteration of the subject as person, not commodity. There is no reform that can tell us our education must not be about some old basics—we are all equal before death and suffering and our need for love and music and real work. No reform should lead us away from the truth that *every* student deserves the right to these truths equally.

This book is an argument that education reform, whose flaws have been so eloquently identified by others, is revealed in its weakness. These stories show the inherent tendency for contemporary education discourse to radically create and alter the individual's perception of him or herself, but not in the direction of enlightenment or any salvation. Teachers and students, consumers of educational discourse, are to remain in thrall of the myths central to the smooth operation of alienation and global working-class competition. These stories are reasonable examples of this verity. Until the vanity and simulated success associated with it are subsumed by

an allegiance to contemplation and the salvation of human personhood, we will be victims of promoters. While education is all
mixed up in some of our great myths, we will not work out the
corrosive effect our allegiance has on the chance for public school,
working-class kids to see beyond their vision of themselves as
suckers, suckers for a good story that is a bad bet. We will stand
on the beach, and though we should know better, we will wait for
the kago to come.

NOTES

1. Jonathan Kozol, *Savage Inequalities* (New York: Harper, 1991); E. D.
Hirsch, *Cultural Literacy: What Every American Needs to Know* (Boston:
Houghton Mifflin, 1987). See Stanley Aronowitz and Henry A. Giroux,
Postmodern Education (Minneapolis: University of Minnesota Press, 1991) for
a discussion of the politics of literacy within the larger reform debate and for
important distinctions between the purposes of Bloom and Hirsch.

2. Hannah Arendt, *The Human Condition* (New York: Doubleday, 1959),
p. 51.

3. Ibid., p. 71.

4. Ibid., p. 153.

5. Ibid., p. 297.

6. Ibid., p. 28.

7. Thomas Merton, *Love and Living*, eds., Naomi B. Stone and Brother
Patrick Hart (New York: Harcourt Brace Jovanovich, 1979), p. 34.

8. Ibid., p. 34.

9. Ibid., p. 17.

10. Ibid.

11. Ibid., p. 81.

12. Ibid., p. 82.

13. Svi Shapiro, *Between Capitalism and Democracy* (New York: Bergin &
Garvey, 1990), p. 131.

14. Merton, *Love and Living*, p. 86.

15. Shapiro, *Between Capitalism*, p. 135.

16. Paul Goodman, *Growing Up Absurd* (New York: Random House, 1960),
p. 8.

17. Ibid., p. 29.

18. Ibid., p. 33.

19. Ibid., p. 29.

20. Ibid., p. 33.

21. Stanley Aronowitz and Henry A. Giroux, *Education under Siege* (South Hadley, Mass.: Bergin & Garvey, 1985), p. 203.

22. Ibid., p. 192.

23. Ibid., p. 165.

24. Goodman, *Growing Up Absurd*, p. 154.

25. Thomas Merton, *Love and Living*, eds., Naomi Stone and Brother Patrick Hart, p. 4.

26. Ibid., p. 5.

27. Ibid.

28. Ibid., p. 17.

29. Ibid., p. 27.

Selected Bibliography

Alic, John A. "Who Designs Work?: Organizing Production in an Age of High Technology." *Technology and Society* 12 (1990): 301–317.

Arendt, Hannah. *The Human Condition.* New York: Doubleday, 1959.

————. *On Violence.* New York: Harcourt Brace, 1970.

Aronowitz, Stanley, and Henry A. Giroux. *Education under Siege.* South Hadley, Mass.: Bergin & Garvey, 1985.

————. *Education Still under Siege.* 2d ed. Westport, Conn.: Bergin & Garvey, 1993.

————. *Postmodern Education.* Minneapolis: University of Minnesota Press, 1991.

Bangsberg, P. T. "Asia Pays High Price for Success as Lax Safety Rules Claim Victims." *Journal of Commerce and Commercial* (May 25, 1993).

Bathrick, David. "Max Schmeling on the Canvas: Boxing as an Icon of Weimar Culture." *New German Critique* (Fall 1990): 113–137.

Becker, Gary S. "The Adam Smith Address: Education, Labor Force Quality and the Economy." *Business Economics* 27, no. 1: 7–12.

Bernstein, Richard J., ed. *Habermas and Modernity.* Cambridge: MIT Press, 1985.

Bershad, Lawrence, and Richard J. Ensor. "Boxing in the U.S.: Reform, Abolition or Federal Control?: A New Jersey Case Study." *Seton Hall Law Review* 19: 865–915.

Beyer, Landon, and George H. Wood. "Critical Inquiry and Moral Action in Education." *Educational Theory* 36, no. 1 (Winter 1986): 9–12.

Bina, Cyrus, and Chuck Davis. "Transnational Capital, the Global Labor Process and the International Labor Movement." In Berch Berberoglu, *The Labor Process and Control of Labor.* Westport, Conn.: Praeger, 1993: 152–170.

Bleecker, Samuel E. "The Information Age Office." *Futurist* (Jan./Feb. 1991): 19–20.

Brosio, Richard. *The Frankfurt School: An Analysis of the Contradictions and Guises of Liberal Capitalist Societies.* Muncie, Ind.: Ball State University Monograph 29, 1980.

Brown, Bruce. *Marx, Freud, and the Critique of Everyday Life.* London: Monthly Review Press, 1973.

Carlsson, Chris, ed. *Bad Attitude: The Processed World Anthology.* London: Verso, 1990.

Carnoy, Martin. "High Technology and Education: An Economist's View." In Steven Tozer and Kenneth D. Benne, eds. *Society as Educator in an Age of Transition.* National Society for the Study of Education. Chicago: University of Chicago Press, 1987.

Cooperman, Saul, and Leo Klagholtz. "New Jersey's Alternate Route to Certification." *Phi Delta Kappan* (June 1985): 691–695.

Cottom, Daniel. *Abyss of Reason: Cultural Movements, Revelations, and Betrayals.* Oxford: University of Oxford Press, 1991.

Ellul, Jacques. *Propaganda: The Formation of Men's Attitudes.* New York: Alfred A. Knopf, 1965.

Entwistle, Harold. *Class, Culture and Education.* Cambridge: Methuen, 1978.

Feynman, Richard P. *What Do You Care What Other People Think?* New York: Bantam Books, 1988.

Fine, Michele. "A Diary on Privatization and on Public Possibilities." *Educational Theory* 43, no. 1 (Winter 1993): 33–39.

Forgacs, David, ed. *An Antonio Gramsci Reader, Selected Writings: 1916–1935.* New York: Schocken Books, 1988.

Fowlie, Wallace. *The Age of Surrealism.* New York: Swallow Press, 1950.

Fox, Richard Wightman, and T. J. Jackson Lears. *The Culture of Consumption: Critical Essays in American History, 1880–1980.* New York: Pantheon, 1983, pp. 177–209.

Garson, Barbara. *The Electronic Sweatshop: How Computers Are Transforming the Office of the Future into the Factory of the Past.* New York: Simon and Schuster, 1988.

Gershman, Herbert S. *The Surrealist Revolution in France.* Ann Arbor: University of Michigan Press, 1969.

Gilbert, James B. *Work Without Salvation: America's Intellectuals and Industrial Alienation.* Baltimore: Johns Hopkins University Press, 1977.

Giroux, Henry. *Border Crossings: Cultural Workers and the Politics of Opposition.* New York: Routledge, 1992.

————. *Disturbing Pleasures: Learning Popular Culture.* New York: Routledge, 1994.

————. *Ideology, Culture and the Process of Schooling.* Philadelphia: Temple University Press, 1981.

————. *Schooling and the Struggle for Public Life: Critical Pedagogy in the Modern Age.* Minneapolis: University of Minnesota Press, 1988.

————. "Theories of Reproduction and Resistance in the New Sociology of Education: A Critical Analysis." *Harvard Educational Review* 53, no. 3 (August 1983): 257–293.

————. *Theory and Resistance in Education: A Pedagogy for the Opposition.* South Hadley, Mass.: Bergin & Garvey, 1983.

Goodman, Paul. *Growing Up Absurd.* New York: Random House, 1960.

Heyman, Steven R. "Ethical Issues in Performance Enhancement Approaches with Amateur Boxers." *The Sport Psychologist* 4 (1990): 48–54.

Hirsch, E. D. *Cultural Literacy: What Every American Needs to Know.* Boston: Houghton Mifflin, 1987.

Hohler, Robert T. *"I Touch the Future . . ."*: *The Story of Christa McAuliffe.* New York: Random House, 1986.

Inglis, Fred. *Cultural Studies.* Oxford: Blackwell, 1993.

Jameson, Frederic. *Marxism and Form.* Princeton: Princeton University Press, 1971.

————. "On Cultural Studies." *Social Text* 34 (Spring 1993): 17–52.

Katz-Fishman, Walda, and Jerome Scott. "The Labor Process and Class Struggle: Political Responses to the Control and Exploitation of Labor." In Berch Berberoglu, *The Labor Process and Control of Labor.* Westport, Conn.: Praeger, 1993, pp. 171–192.

Kellner, Douglas. *Critical Theory, Marxism, and Modernity.* Baltimore: Johns Hopkins University Press, 1989.

————. *Jean Baudrillard: From Marxism to Postmodernism and Beyond.* Stanford, Calif.: Stanford University Press, 1989.

Kozol, Jonathan. *Savage Inequalities.* New York: Harper, 1991.

Landsberger, Henry A. *Hawthorne Revisited: "Management and the Worker" Its Critics and Developments in Human Relations in Industry.* Ithaca: Cornell University Press, 1958.

Lembke, Jerry. "Class Formation and Class Capacities: A New Approach to the Study of Labor and the Labor Process." In Berch Berberoglu, *The Labor Process and Control of Labor.* Westport, Conn.: Praeger, 1993, pp. 1–20.

Lewis, Helena. *The Politics of Surrealism.* New York: Paragon, 1988.

McConnell, Malcolm. *Challenger: A Major Malfunction.* Garden City, New York: Doubleday, 1987.

McLaren, Peter. *Life in Schools.* New York: Longman, 1989.

130   Selected Bibliography

————. *Schooling as a Ritual Performance*. London: Routledge & Kegan Paul, 1986.

Mailer, Norman. *The Fight*. Boston: Little, Brown and Co., 1975.

Marcuse, Herbert. *Counterrevolution and Revolt*. Boston: Beacon Press, 1972.

Marien, Michael. "The Two Visions of Post-Industrial Society." *Futures* (October 1977): 415–431.

Massumi, Brian. *A User's Guide to "Capitalism and Schizophrenia."* Cambridge: MIT Press, 1992.

Merton, Thomas. *Love and Living*. Ed. Naomi B. Stone and Brother Patrick Hart. New York: Harcourt Brace Jovanovich, 1979.

Nadeau, Maurice. *The History of Surrealism*. Cambridge: Harvard University Press, 1989.

Oates, Joyce Carol. *On Boxing*. New York: Doubleday, 1987.

Oates, Joyce Carol, and Daniel Halpern, eds. *Reading the Fights*. New York: Henry Holt and Co., 1988.

Parker, Robert E. "The Labor Force in Transition: Growth of the Contingent Workforce in the United States." In Berch Berberoglu, *The Labor Process and Control of Labor*. Westport, Conn.: Praeger, 1993, pp. 116–136.

Peters, Charles. "From Ouagadougou to Cape Canaveral: Why the Bad News Doesn't Travel Up." *The Washington Monthly* (April 1986): 27–31.

Purpel, David. *The Moral and Spiritual Crisis in Education: A Curriculum for Justice and Compassion in Education*. New York: Bergin & Garvey, 1989.

Reitman, Sanford. *The Educational Messiah Complex*. Sacramento, CA: Caddo Gap Press, 1992.

Report of the Presidential Commission on the Space Shuttle Challenger *Accident*. Washington, D.C.: 1986, p. 89.

Roethlisberger, F. J., and William J. Dickson. *Management and the Worker*. New York: John Wiley and Sons, Inc., 1964.

Rosemont, Franklin. *André Breton: What Is Surrealism*. New York: Monad, 1978.

Sandrow, Nahma. *Surrealism: Theater, Arts and Ideas*. New York: Harper and Row, 1972.

Scheck, Dennis C. "High Technology: Job Skill Requirements and Job Opportunities." *Humanity and Society* 11, no. 3 (1987): 152–163.

Schoenberger, Erica. "The Ambiguous Future of Professional and Technical Workers in Manufacturing: Some Hypotheses." *Acta Sociologica* 31, no. 3 (1988): 241–247.

Shapiro, Svi. *Between Capitalism and Democracy: Educational Policy and the Crisis of the Welfare State*. New York: Bergin & Garvey, 1990.

————. "Beyond the Sociology of Education: Culture, Politics and the Promise of Educational Change." *Educational Theory* 38, no. 4 (Fall 1988): 415–430.

Shea, Christine M. "Pentagon vs. Multinational Capitalism: The Political Economy of the 1980's School Reform Movement." In Christine M. Shea, Ernest Kahane, and Peter Sola, eds., *The New Servants of Power: A Critique of the 1980's School Reform Movement.* New York: Praeger, 1990, p. 19.

Shea, Christine M., Ernest Kahane, and Peter Sola, eds., *The New Servants of Power: A Critique of the 1980's School Reform Movement.* New York: Praeger, 1989.

Snauwaert, Dale T. "Reclaiming the Lost Treasure: Deliberation and Strong Democratic Education." *Educational Theory* 42, no. 3 (Summer 1992): 351–367.

Stirk, Peter M. R. *Max Horkheimer: A New Interpretation.* Lanham, Maryland: Barnes and Noble, 1992.

Tanzer, Andrew. "Cantonese Conquistadores." *Forbes Magazine* (March 2, 1992): 56–58.

Thompson, E. P. "Homage to Thomas McGrath." In *Triquarterly*, issue *Thomas McGrath: Life and the Poem* (Fall 1987).

U.S. House Committee on Education and Labor. Subcommittee on Labor Standards. *The Federal Boxing Protection Act of 1983.* H.R. 751. 98th Cong., 1st sess., 5 May 1983.

U.S. House Committee on Energy and Commerce. Subcommittee on Commerce, Transportation and Tourism. *Hearings on H.R. 1778*, bill to establish a Congressional advisory commission on boxing, 98th Cong., 1st sess., 15 February 1983 and 18 March 1983.

————. *Hearings on H.R. 1705*, bill to promote health and safety in professional boxing, 99th Cong., 1st sess., 30 July 1985.

Waldberg, Patrick. *Surrealism.* New York: Oxford University Press, 1965.

Wiley, Ralph. *Serenity: A Boxing Memoir.* New York: Henry Holt and Co., 1989.

Index

ABOUT THE AUTHORS

GUY SENESE is Associate Professor of Educational Foundations in the Department of Leadership and Educational Policy Studies at Northern Illinois University. He is the author of *Self-Determination and the Social Education of Native Americans* (Praeger, 1991) and co-author, with Steven Tozer and Paul Violas, of *School and Society: Educational Practice as Social Expression* (1992).

RALPH PAGE is Associate Professor of Philosophy of Education in the Department of Educational Policy Studies at the University of Illinois at Urbana-Champaign.

ISBN 0-89789-402-2

9 780897 894029

90000>

EAN

HARDCOVER BAR CODE

83   10